Unlocking Sustainable Cities

Radical Geography

Series Editors:
Danny Dorling, Matthew T. Huber and Jenny Pickerill
Former editor: Kate Derickson

Also available:

In Their Place
The Imagined Geographies of Poverty
Stephen Crossley

Making Workers
Radical Geographies of Education
Katharyne Mitchell

Space Invaders
Radical Geographies of Protest
Paul Routledge

New Borders
Migration, Hotspots and
the European Superstate
Antonis Vradis, Evie Papada,
Joe Painter and Anna Papoutsi

Unlocking Sustainable Cities

A Manifesto for Real Change

Paul Chatterton

PLUTO PRESS

First published 2019 by Pluto Press
345 Archway Road, London N6 5AA

www.plutobooks.com

British Library Cataloguing in Publication Data
A catalogue record for this book is available from the British Library

ISBN   978 0 7453 3702 9   Hardback
ISBN   978 0 7453 3701 2   Paperback
ISBN   978 1 7868 0363 4   PDF eBook
ISBN   978 1 7868 0365 8   Kindle eBook
ISBN   978 1 7868 0364 1   EPUB eBook

This book is printed on paper suitable for recycling and made from fully
managed and sustained forest sources. Logging, pulping and manufacturing
processes are expected to conform to the environmental standards of the
country of origin.

Typeset by Stanford DTP Services, Northampton, England

Simultaneously printed in the United Kingdom and United States of America

Dedicated to all those who know
we can still make a difference

Contents

Acknowledgements

There are many people I would like to thank for helping to shape this book. First, I would like to thank the Series Editors and especially Danny Dorling and Jenny Pickerill for encouraging me to write this book in the first place. At Pluto Press, David Castle, Robert Webb and Melanie Patrick have offered fantastic encouragement and support and deserve respect for backing this radical geography book series.

Second, I would like to offer special thanks to two of my recent PhD students, Rebecca Sumerling and Stella Darby. Both dedicated substantial time providing some excellent case studies, which helped bring this book to life. I would also like to thank Stella for her editing assistance.

Third, I would like to thank my colleague James McKay, who is the Manager of the Doctoral Training Centre in Low Carbon Technologies at the University of Leeds. James provided the excellent line illustrations for the book and its cover. These build on James' inspirational graphic novel *Dreams of a Low Carbon Future*.[1] For my own book, James created illustrations that represent the topics of the four chapters, and they all take their cue from how our own city, Leeds, could be transformed. The Car-Free City illustration is loosely based on how the Leeds waterfront area could look after the age of cars; the Post-Carbon City illustration radically reconfigures one of the libraries at the University of Leeds as a sustainable, zero energy building; the Bio City illustration is loosely based on the Leeds skyline, substantially altered through a closer relationship to nature; and the Common City illustration is based on what could happen in the dense Victorian back-to-back housing around the city, if our neighbourhoods were reconfigured through the prisms of direct democracy and community wealth building.

I am also indebted to all the projects I am involved in that continue to inspire and motivate me to work towards transformative change: LILAC co-housing cooperative, Kirkstall Valley Development Trust and Leeds Community Homes, to name a few. Thanks also to colleagues at the School of Geography, the Cities research theme and the MSc in Sustainable Cities, all at the University of Leeds, for their support and input. Finally, as ever, huge thanks to my loving partner Tash, who reminds me how to keep motivated and committed to social change, and my two young sons, who are a constant reminder of why a book like this is so necessary.

Series Preface

The Radical Geography series consists of accessible books which use geographical perspectives to understand issues of social and political concern. These short books include critiques of existing government policies and alternatives to staid ways of thinking about our societies. They feature stories of radical social and political activism, guides to achieving change, and arguments about why we need to think differently on many contemporary issues, if we are to live better together on this planet.

A geographical perspective involves seeing the connections within and between places, as well as considering the role of space and scale to develop a new and better understanding of current problems. Written largely by academic geographers, books in the series deliberately target issues of political, environmental and social concern. The series showcases clear explications of geographical approaches to social problems, and it has a particular interest in action currently being undertaken to achieve positive change that is radical, achievable, real and relevant.

The target audience ranges from undergraduates to experienced scholars, as well as from activists to conventional policy makers, but these books are also for people interested in the world, who do not already have a radical outlook and who want to be engaged and informed by a short, well-written and thought-provoking book.

Danny Dorling, Matthew T. Huber and Jenny Pickerill
Series Editors

Introduction

In Detroit, Philadelphia and New Orleans, groups of people have set up Urban Consulates, a network of parlours for residents seeking urban exchange. In Liverpool, Granby Workshop has grown out of community-led neighbourhood rebuilding and makes experimental hand-made products. In Indianapolis, People for Urban Progress take unwanted goods and recycle them into items that contribute to the public good. In Berkeley, HackerMoms is the first-ever women's hacker-space, a collaborative space where do it your selfers share tools, intelligence and community. In Leeds, Playful Anywhere incubates, develops and designs playful participatory projects putting people and play at the heart of public engagement and place. In Mexico City, the Miravalle Community Council has transformed abandoned public spaces in marginalised communities through establishing libraries, low-budget lunch rooms, health and recreational centres and recycling facilities. In Dallas, the Better Block Foundation is developing open-source solutions to help cities, community groups and emerging leaders create rapid prototyping in the service of creative place-making and support of public life. In Rotterdam, Buurtflirt's (literally, Neighbourhood Flirts) develop temporary, creative meeting points in forgotten locations in the city, bringing people together for social action. In Buenos Aries, the cartoneros (or informal litter pickers) have created stable cooperative work opportunities for the city's most marginalised. In Oregon, the Walk [Your City] project encourages walking to tackle auto-dependency and community activists have covered the city with signs promoting walking and cycling routes. The Vancouver Public Space Network has developed projects to tackle the growing corporatisation of space and promote alternatives to it, such as community gardens, walkable communities and billboard activism.[1]

This list of inspiring examples could go on. Something largely unnoticed is happening in cities across the world. There are countless projects where people from all walks of life and city sectors are creating, resisting and intervening in their unfolding urban story. In spite of the overbearing weight of corporate power, loss of public space, bureaucratic hierarchies, ingrained inequalities and even the presence of war and violence, people and projects are emerging to lay down markers for very different urban futures. They are unlocking the huge untapped potential of sustainable cities. They may be partial, small scale and ephemeral. Efforts might not have the answers to urban poverty, inequality or climate change, but they represent a swarm of civic innovation, seeking to harness potential wherever they see it. This is a constellation of activity, a many-headed hydra that takes inspiration from activities on the other side of the world as much as from next door. They represent a healthy, radical understanding and critique of business-as-usual urbanism that is pushing cities to their social, ecological and economic limits. They are sceptical of whether techno-fixes and smart digital solutions on their own can be urban saviours.

WHERE TO START?

So why focus on cities? It is now well known that the majority of humanity on our planet live in cities and that over the next few years urban society will account for about three-quarters of total energy use and greenhouse gas emissions. Behind these headlines, there is a stark and disturbing agenda. It is a call to action about the very survival of our species and the ecosystems that we depend upon. For anyone intervening in how cities may unfold in the future, there are a whole host of complex and persistent problems that require urgent attention: climate resilience and adaptation; biodiversity and ecosystem protection; reductions in fossil fuel dependency; ensuring decent levels of prosperity and well-being; tackling generations of worklessness and poverty, building institutions that empower and enable; ensuring equality in terms of outcomes and procedures; figuring out how to incentivise changes in social practices; safeguarding children and vulnerable adults, reorienting work and education towards the challenges that lie ahead; and developing the financial, institutional and cultural shifts needed to underpin it all.[2]

To confound this, there is no agreed view on the task ahead. Interventions in future challenges are framed by how we see, and are positioned, in the world. A view of urban change and priorities for action from Bangladesh, for example, is radically different from those for Bradford or Boston. For some, urban sustainability challenges may mean avoiding death at the hands of an occupying army or scavenging for food and basic resources. For others, it might mean improving road safety or air pollution or using data to make public transport more efficient. At first glance, it is hard to see what links these. They emerge from very different social, material and geopolitical circumstances. But digging deeper, we find common threads: a desire to develop alternatives to old paradigm urbanism, ingrained bureaucracies, corporate power and disconnected governments that have taken the control of cities out of the hands of its citizens.

This is not yet another book about sustainable, low-carbon, climate-friendly or resilient cities. It is intended as a manifesto for unlocking sustainable cities through what I purposefully call a manifesto for real change. This contrasts to many of the false solutions, weak promises and blind alleys masquerading as real change. I use the term real rather than radical, as this book is about transformative action that is also within our reach. As I explain in the coming pages, central to my theory of change is working towards sustainable cities through unlocking the great potential that comes from countless acts of transformative and disruptive civic innovation. But, at the same time, it requires the prevention of locking into dead-end routes or short-term gains and locking down socially and environmentally regressive tendencies that seek to privatise, commodify and individualise city life.

In particular, the book foregrounds the fact that one of the central problems is the way that we approach the very idea of sustainability. The concept of sustainable development has become so well worn that it has become meaningless. It largely concerns sustaining the status quo through a basket of reforms and a naive faith in the power of new socio-technical arrangements. Real sustainability can only be worked towards by embarking upon a deep and painful questioning, pulling apart and reorienting the dominant urban project of the human species during late capitalism's anthropocene.[3]

At a practical level, for cities, this is a serious call for radical action and is a fundamental step change in urban policy, institutions and action. Our cities are at a junction point. A generational challenge, and opportunity, is ahead. We need ideas, policy and action that can lay down radically different urban futures – those based on equality, prosperity and sustainability, but that also respond realistically to the enormity and interconnected complexities of the challenges ahead. Therefore, this book is not radical for the sake of being radical. Given the challenges we face, I'm reminded of the old anarchist saying, 'be realistic, demand the impossible'.

This is not a book that seeks solutions from top-down corporate-led, business-as-usual models, nor one that naively celebrates the power of small grass-roots projects, the power of a resurgent radical local state or lone mavericks who can break through old paradigms. Rather, it seeks to explore the power of rapidly emerging constellations of connected experiments that sit between and within all of these – that can harness the creative power of the many and have the potential to radically unlock the latent potential of cities. In particular, what these civic innovators point towards is institutional building that connects bottom-up and top-down change. Some of the most transformative innovation is occurring in this middle out or meso level.[4]

Responses, then, are multiple, contradictory and only partially clear. Are we trying to work with existing structures and institutions, set up utopian examples far away from them or confront and break them through more direct resistance? This book sits in the middle of these debates, for which there are no easy answers. Echoing the sentiment of political writer and activist John Holloway, action needs to be simultaneously in, against and beyond the contemporary city.[5] *Unlocking Sustainable Cities*, then, is a critical yet hopeful journey through what progressive urban futures might entail. It is a journey wrought with problems and contradictions, and at times, it will feel uncomfortable. The intention is not to provide a complete synthesis or road map to some utopian sustainable city, but to work with its complexity and messiness as essential resources.

UNLOCKING REAL CHANGE IN SUSTAINABLE CITIES

We need to begin with the problematic of approaching different visions of possible urban futures as well as road maps to get there. A variety of visions are pitched, often against each other, ranging from the prospect of future conflict and collapse, liberatory or utopian transformation, business as usual, as well as technocratic-led ecological modernisation and renewal. Contained within these debates are assumptions and struggles over very different forms of social relations, agencies and power structures, deployments of technologies, levels of corporate control, institutional realignment, values and forms of governance, and changes in social practices. In particular, different visions of the future contain assumptions about what needs to be promoted and demoted, created and resisted.

I frame this whole book through a dual movement: to lock down and unlock. First, I point towards the need for resistance and action in the face of aspects of urban life that need to be locked down to avoid damaging and unsafe versions of urban sustainability. Many features of the contemporary city have become bound up with unproductive and wasteful options. Think of moves to automated cars rather than a wholesale shift away from automobile dependency; centralised and corporate controlled low(er) carbon energy systems rather than localised, green civic energy; mass eco-city developments rather than integrated, affordable, green infrastructures; corporate control of land rather than the creation of common resources; and a focus on digital innovation at the expense of material inequalities. As we seek to unlock potential, we must not forget the task of locking down what is damaging.

Second, there needs to be a process of creation to enable and empower, or unlock, a whole parallel series of practices and institutions that foster greater levels of environmental sustainability, social justice and economic equality. The idea of unlocking is a powerful metaphor for our times. Huge civic potential is bubbling under the surface, but is constrained through a whole host of complex mechanisms related to power, greed, fear, paternalism, division, mistrust, the unevenness of educational opportunities, resources and social networks. Unlocking includes simple everyday tasks such as building social connections and speaking up for how things could be different, and more formal and complex tasks such as fighting for more resources and legislative changes. These activities which unlock, replicate and spread potential are the major focus of this book.

This process of unlocking and lock-down is not easy or straight-forward. One person's problem is another person's solution. Cities are literally full of power and politics and any process of change that is substantial and transformative will entail differences and conflicts between vested interests, as well as overcoming social and institutional inertia. Given the complexity of our social world, there is little certainty in terms of outcomes and there is an important element of watching and waiting for emergent properties. This landscape is peppered with unintended consequences and perverse outcomes. Causality is thrown into disarray.[6] Indeed, we need to watch for alternatives, which might not turn out to be real alternatives at all. Real choice comes from the ability to direct finances, control resources, make and scrutinise decisions, and steer the planning system. In the conclusion, I explore some broader issues of urban movement building, strategies and tactics against this backdrop of greater urban complexity.

FIVE THEMES FOR REAL CHANGE

I use five themes that shape and guide this great process of unlocking sustainable urban futures: compassion, imagination, experimentation, co-production and transformation. In some way, all the examples I explore in this book illuminate these themes.

The first is compassion and the urgent need to inject empathy, shared understanding and solidarity into the way we construct city futures. Compassion is commonly defined as a sensitivity to suffering of oneself and others with a commitment to try to alleviate and prevent it.[7] What would this mean for how we approach sustainability in cities? If we regard cities as connected and complex ecologies of people, resources, artefacts and infrastructures, then we start to understand the need for a compassionate approach to our daily lives. We have all simply found ourselves here, dealing with our own pasts and doing the best we can. But the conditions for compassion are being further eroded. Intense individualisation, performance and reward cultures and status anxieties built into fast-paced urban living blinds us to the needs of those around us. A compassionate city is also a slower city.[8] More humane, durable and legible solutions to an increasingly complex urban world can be better explored by slowing down.

Moreover, the contemporary ecological and social footprint of a city connects us to a complex range of people and places. An appreciation of these diverse links is a starting point for creating greater compassion and an ethics of care for distant others: the coffee plantation worker, the Thai seamstress, the Bolivian tin miner, the Korean microchip maker. What responsibility do we have to them? How do we unravel these connections? Similarly, a broader sense of ethics means challenging local and national governments, local elites and organisations implicated in all this. Knowing your local elite and how they operate is key to understanding how a city is run – and in whose interests. In every locality, we can unravel how firms, institutions and universities create and perpetuate webs of inequality. Structural patterns of inequalities from legacies of imperialism and colonialism continue to shape urbanity in such profound and largely invisible ways. In this context, compassion also means recognising these uneven historical geographies and finding ways to cross and connect these social and spatial lines of inequality that divide cities.

The second theme is imagination, and the need to envisage the urban, which might seem impossible beyond the current frame of reference.[9] Sustainable cities emerge as much through locking down and unlocking various imaginative tendencies as material ones. Which imaginations, or narratives and stories about the future, gain traction will determine the kind of futures that become more likely. In this terrain of speculation, advocacy and imagination, a hopeful approach becomes a useful antidote to the despondencies of our age. The writer and activist Rebecca Solnit has called this: finding hope in the dark.[10] There are so many urban problems and pathologies that shape our thinking and action. Not only do we need rapid structural material changes that address these, but we also need to hopefully reimagine what a more prosperous and sustainable urban life could be like. Solnit's work is part of a broader tradition that rejects top-down thinking and linear relations. She encourages us to find hope in everyday actions, and stresses that we are making history all the time.[11] In this reimagining of sustainable cities, the means are as important as the endpoints.

In a context of a mounting sense of uncertainty around climate breakdown, energy security, migration, permanent war or the future of public services, it is easy to fall back on familiar hierarchical command and control ways of being and doing – but it becomes especially important that we do not retreat from freedom and imagination. They will be the lifeblood of opening up opportunities for more empowering, collaborative forms of action that can unlock and successfully respond to the challenges ahead.

This reimagining process has become a battleground between different political voices on the left and right. Developing the kinds of sustainable cities we want to see will require acknowledging but not getting caught up in these differences, and creating common sense arguments that weave together what needs to be locked down and unlocked into convincing and inclusive storylines. There are no easy answers or blueprints – and nor should there be. Along the way, there will be ideas and values that might be uncomfortable and unmanageable, but that is the rawness and energy of being involved in social change. Feasibility is important, however. Novel ideas have to be accessible, inspiring and viable, but have to make the status quo look absurd. Incremental steps which prefigure future changes are likely to provide traction. Moreover, humour, play and satire will have a key role. For example, studies have shown that the imagination and creative play that we use during childhood is an incredibly important base for future adult creative potential.[12] Encouraging greater play in our future cities then is one of the great ingredients of creating a more compassionate, active and imaginative citizenry.[13]

Moreover, education is key to harnessing imagination in ways that create practical steps for action. Learning about workable alternatives, providing practical exercises and resources, helping with action planning and campaign building can all help. Educators take on the responsibility of guiding groups beyond common fears to reveal answers and exit routes, and laying possible options on the table. Essential is the ability to make connections and establish bridges between people's everyday realities and what they can start to think is possible in the future. Hence, different options are presented slowly and gradually, with honest reflection, compromise and set backs along the way. Part of the learning experience is sharing what is feasible. Ways of urban living beyond the status quo already exist. On their own, they may seem weak or irrelevant, but gathered up and presented and experienced collectively, they can provide excitement and hope for an achievable creative, empowered life.

The third is experimentation, and the need to take bold action to explore novel possibilities through radical forms of prototyping and exploration beyond the business-as-usual approach. The term experimentation traditionally refers to the more common act of experimenting undertaken to verify or falsify hypotheses between phenomena in controlled environments. However, lab experiments have never been the removed places that traditional images of men in white coats might evoke. They are in fact highly open and negotiated spaces – far from being immune to external pressures, they are indelibly mixed up with the outside world. Cities, as complex systems represent something similar – almost live field experiments.[14] Flows of people and resources constantly come together in novel ways to experiment with different arrangements and possible outcomes. Given the stalemate of policy in the face of the scale of the challenges, creating zones of experimentation offers great opportunities for: entering into the flow of city life to insert novel and disruptive values and habits; and then observing, analysing and evaluating the outcomes, and how they can destabilise the status quo.

As I explore in Chapter 4, city labs represent a commitment to this kind of experimentation, generating knowledge in new ways, via citizen engagement, co-production and partnerships. These share in common a vision of cities as novel open-experimentation platforms for meeting the grand challenges of our age, such as climate adaptation and mitigation, energy scarcity, financial austerity or social unrest. This is especially pertinent in an increasingly globalised and interconnected age. Cities are the sites of disruptive innovations at various scales, from the neighbourhood to the city-region and beyond. Such disruptive innovations can take many forms: novel horizontal institutions, decentralised neighbourhood organising, land occupations or indeed organising to protect frontline public services.

There are also dangers of open experimentation in cities. Consistency, durability and repetition are also crucial to many of the aspects which allow us to flourish such as reliable transit systems or welfare services. Moreover, there is a danger that experimentation could depoliticise discourse and action, if it becomes overly associated with detached technocrats attempting to orchestrate people and resources or identifying and fixing certain inputs, as well as relying on a naive local bounded politics of scale, where everything that happens in the city can be controlled by the city. While we take an experimental attitude to unlocking sustainable cities, we need to keep in mind the longer-standing traditions of redistributive politics and social inequalities. In particular, we need to establish who is doing the experimenting, to what ends and who will control the outputs. We need experiments that solve perceived societal crises but in ways that foreground equality, openness and social justice rather than the free market.

The fourth aspect is co-production and the need to harness collaborative forms of co-working and co-design to urban problem-solving. Co-production is a term which has risen to recent prominence amongst academics and practitioners, and which is used in a range of areas, including the provision of services and goods, as well as research and working practices. Its basic contours relate to a deep commitment to: equality and equal participation; developing shared learning and understanding; building bridges between different institutional contexts and positionalities (especially academic and non-academic, public and private, communities and institutions); developing shared understandings and responsibilities for problem-solving and service delivery; and attempting to find novel solutions to persistent problems. Co-production normally assumes mutual respect, reduced hierarchies between different knowledge contributions, fluid and permeable disciplinary and professional boundaries, and a normative concern with action. It provides opportunities to explore and test knowledge in the context where implementation will take place. Co-production redefines relationships from being extractive or transactional to being interactive. There is a collaborative, iterative process of shared learning. Co-production can help to democratise how we research and in turn lead to socially just change and greater public benefit.[15]

Co-production in cities is flourishing as there is a growing recognition that no single institution has the capacity to diagnose challenges and solve problems on their own. In this context, radically different institutional personas and forms of knowledge production are needed. This opens up participants to a different emotional register, based on vulnerability, partial knowledge and compassion. Co-production flourishes in novel institutions that avoid dichotomies such as public and private and bottom-up or top-down. Sustainable cities, then, will require drastic institutional reinvention as different sectors and citizens come together in novel ways.

The fifth, and perhaps most significant, theme is transformation and a commitment to feasible changes beyond the current paradigm of carbon-dependent and pro-growth economics as the structural conditions that reproduce urban inequality and injustice. Urban society is running out of options to merely 'adjust', and therefore has to look into options for deliberate transformation in the face of multiple crises. This will involve naming and confronting power as well as the historic structural tendencies that continue to shape our world across, such as imperialism, race, class, ethnicity, sexuality and gender.

Moreover, we need to situate the various choices embedded in unlocking sustainable cities within the long-standing critiques of urban industrial society, especially in the context of a rapidly globalised and urban world. Since the 1972 *Limits to Growth* report and the foundational work of E.F. Schumacher,[16] a body of thought and action has emerged across the globe, which presents a sustained argument against globalised and neoliberal urban growth.[17] What we can take from these debates is a need to set a course for progressive urban futures beyond business-as-usual capitalist growth, towards a radically different localised, egalitarian, participatory and people-centred vision for human development. Cities which are more environmentally sustainable are all well and good.

However, the real challenge is to unlock a radically different set of potentials which tackle the underlying mechanisms that perpetuate our uneven world.

FOUR SUSTAINABLE CITY SYSTEMS

My second line of analysis relates to four recognisable features of city life (transport, energy, nature, community) and how each can be transformed: how potential can be unlocked, how lock-in can be avoided, and how unproductive tendencies can be locked down. I call these 'city systems' in the sense that they represent a complex network of people, institutions, practices, cultures, resources and histories that come together in particular places to make things work in certain ways. There are others that I could have focused on but, due to space constraints, the four I have chosen represent basic systems of provision that people depend upon for their daily lives. For each, I foreground the dire consequences of maintaining a business-as-usual approach, and offer jumping off points for developing radical but practical alternatives which have been implemented in particular places and which could be implemented elsewhere. Rather than looking at these areas in silos, we can explore how they work together as part of an integrated urban 'system of systems'. Interventions do not simply affect or influence single areas of urban life. For example, new energy systems bring into play issues of finance and community engagement, food opens up areas of change in land and democracy, mobility is shaped by the kinds of economies and leisure patterns we build, urban greenspaces underpin our health and well-being, and our approach to place-making reflects the relationship to the corporate world.

These urban systems do not make up a complete blueprint, but rather are a set of inspirations, examples, prototypes and tendencies that need to be explored, promoted and embedded. I have kept my perspective and analysis on these topics fairly broad. Therefore, this book will be of interest to students, researchers and teachers in a whole host of disciplines including geography, social and environmental science, civil engineering, economics, community and urban planning, architecture and design. It will also be of interest to urban planners, policy makers and innovators themselves, be they in the private or civil society sectors. Since the momentum to unlock potential in cities is truly global, I have tried to find and explore examples from across the world, which point towards activating novel forms of urban sustainability. Given that it is impossible to have first-hand experience of everything I mention, these portraits are only partial. Where I have missed important events or initiatives, I would love to hear from readers about their reflections and additions. Below I sketch out these four city systems that will form the basis for the following chapters of this book.

The Car-Free City

The nature of urban life is increasingly shaped by how people move around, but it is also increasingly shaped through its lock into fossil fuel based transport. I have chosen to start with this city system as almost all modern ills can be told through the automobile. Cars inflict so many multiple and complicated problems on cities (pollution, road deaths, alienated streets, individualism, unequal access, debt, corporate control, consumerism) that a radical break is needed. Great faith is placed on new technologies such as semi-automated, driverless and hydrogen vehicles that could cut pollution and road deaths and create an efficient, rational transport utopia. But cities full of driverless cars will not stop the descent into alienated street life, status anxiety, debt and corporate-controlled consumerism. Unlocking real change requires a radical break from the whole culture of the car.

In the chapter on Car-Free Cities, I explore a wealth of examples that point to unlocking a very different approach to mobility. As we lock down fossil fuel based transport, we need to unlock the car-free city on a mass scale: cycle lanes, pedestrian routes, mass accessible rapid transport, renewed street life and car-lite urban design. Moreover, the very need for such intense mobility needs to be unpacked and precious urban space simply needs to be reallocated away from motorised vehicles on a huge scale. Unlocking alternative transport futures can only go hand in hand with a shift in planning and zoning, eroding the need for mass, wasteful commuting from neighbourhood to central work zones. Central areas need to be dispersed, work needs to be more broadly distributed, and food, leisure and retail needs rescaling and decoupling from car use. Starting with the car may seem parochial, but it points to the multiple steps to unlocking real change for sustainable cities.

The Post-Carbon City

Cities are locked into an ageing energy system unfit for the challenges ahead. Through their buildings, transport, and producer and consumer services, cities are vast energy users, with high energetic throughputs. All this results in localised pollution, dependence on fossil fuels and significant contributions to greenhouse gas emissions. While there is a push to decarbonise urban energy, it remains locked into outdated, centralised and privatised energy and fossil fuel sources. But under the surface, there is a civic energy revolution forming. Distributed energy networks, local smart grids and micro-generation all point to how cities can unlock zero-carbon pathways.

As I explore in Chapter 2, this is a Post-Carbon City agenda beyond the geopolitical age of oil, gas and coal. It's not just a technical or infrastructure transition but it also entails widespread change in cultural and social practices. The creation and provision of energy needs reconceptualising around a different set of values. In our energy bloated and incredibly unequal urban societies, demand reduction, curtailment and redistribution loom large. Energy remunicipalisation is on the agenda as cities pave the way to provide affordable green energy for their citizens. In this chapter, I explore this new urban energy constellation, how it is starting to work and the rocky road that lies ahead in terms of taking on corporate energy giants, ensuring radical decarbonisation as well as equality.

The Bio City

The ecosystems that cities depend upon are being intensely degraded and the very idea of cities as natural places is now deeply questionable. Given the biospheric, biodiversity and climatic threats ahead, efforts need to focus on the lock-down of ecosystem degradation, resource depletion and the commodification of nature and natural resources. We urgently need to create climate-safe and resilient cities, and in ways that ensure a new basis for human development and social equality.

More fundamentally, the separation between the natural and the urban world is counter-productive. Urban areas are complex constellations of human resources and natural ecosystems. There needs to be a transformation in the relationship between the natural and urban realm and a new human–nature deal based on equality, stewardship, ecological restoration and non-commodified relations. In Chapter 3 on the Bio City, I explore unlocking these emerging trends through a radical emerging approach to urban nature including urban rewilding, permaculture, biomimicry, biophilia, urban agriculture, continuous productive urban landscapes and blue-green infrastructure.

The Common City

Finally, in Chapter 4, I explore the idea of the Common City through innovations in community place-making, economics and democracy. The physical places, the actual land and territories we live on and occupy, give us a sense of place, sustain us and provide well-being and shelter. However, place-making has been subject to abstract and alienated planning systems, scarred by bureaucracy, corporate greed and concentrated land ownership. Moreover, urban economies have increasingly become locked into fast money, volatile inward investment, domination by big brands, zero-hour contracts and low pay, poor skills and educational opportunities. Much of this isn't geared towards the challenges ahead, but instead instrumentally feeds extra-local economies and firms, extracting surplus value from places and stripping them of their essential resources. And to confound this, contemporary forms of urban democracy and governance are intensely unequal and hierarchical. In the global North, city governments are rarely governed beyond an established party political elite, while city or metro mayors have done little to radically decentralise power to neighbourhoods. More worryingly, urban dwellers in many parts of the majority world live in fear of occupation, paramilitaries and war.

The common city points to a fundamental shift in the way that place-making, urban economies and democracy are undertaken. These come in many guises: novel forms of citizen-led housing, community ownership, localised and solidarity-based economics, collaborative production, local currencies and civic finance. Moreover, radically new ways of doing democracy need activating not only through experiments in popular assemblies, participatory budgets, citizens forums, distributed networks, co-production and cooperatives but also through the use of civil disobedience and direct action as ways to call attention to injustices.

* * *

Together these city systems create an agenda for a car-free, post-carbon, commons-based bio city. This is an ambitious and incomplete agenda that explores how innovators are unlocking cities from automobile dependency, embarking on the shift from private, fossil fuel vehicles towards zero-carbon urbanism, restoring urban nature by moving away from ecologically damaging industrialisation, and unleashing locally responsive economies and renewed democratic participation. I conclude the book with some strategic reflections. If any of this potential is to be unlocked, we have to think big, act small and start now. We have to get organised and confront the challenges of how this great unlocking of real urban sustainability can be achieved and replicated. And since this book is intended to be a manifesto, I end the book by offering some suggestions for real action and change.

1

The Car-Free City

My exploration of unlocking sustainable cities begins with the car. This might seem an odd, slightly parochial and technical place to begin. Why cars? Surely the future to unlocking urban sustainability doesn't simply reside here? But how we have chosen to design transport systems touches almost all areas of city life. Debating how city dwellers undertake the mundane and taken for granted task of getting around opens up further conversations about how we see ourselves and our fellow citizens, where and how we work, shop and play, the health of our children, how safe we feel, what we can afford, and our impact on air, climate and water systems. The mere act of moving around cities provides a detailed window to view the problems and opportunities faced by urban areas in the future.

This chapter, then, is about much more than the car. It's about urban mobility and everything that it impacts upon. I focus on the urgent task of how and why we need to lock down the car-based city. Almost all modern ills can be told through the rise of the private fossil fuel powered automobile: unnecessary road deaths, the global pandemic of urban air pollution, mounting greenhouse gas emissions, geopolitical wars, the concentration of corporate wealth and mounting consumer debt, depression, status anxiety, obesity, alienated streetscapes, the decline of vibrant public life and the corrosive effects of individualism (we are all too familiar with road rage, predatory driving and traffic tantrums). I also focus on unlocking the car-free city, or at least how we begin the steps towards weaning ourselves away from it. We are not simply addressing the technical issues of designing and building alternative mobility options, although of course these are essential. As I explore in this chapter, issues of culture, infrastructure, work, organisation, behaviour, finance, marketing, power and politics instantly rise to the surface. How we choose to get around the city is a set of choices about the very future of the city itself.

CAR CULTURE: HOW DID WE GET INTO THIS MESS?

In 1898, at the world's first international urban planning conference, some attendees predicted that manure left behind by horses pulling coaches and wagons would soon pile up to the upper floors of New York City buildings. Of course, for those worrying about horse waste on city streets the rapid arrival of the motorised private car changed the entire issue. In a similar way, today we are left wondering what might happen to our cities if the growth of cars is left unchecked. We are hoping that there is something on the horizon, a magic bullet that will solve the problem: zero-emission vehicles; driverless cars; frictionless transportation pods. Who knows? But before we rush into the soft comfort of futurist speculation, it's worth just reversing up a bit and taking a sober look at how we got here, what we are up against and how we might take a different course.

We are facing no less than a car 'industrial–political–cultural' complex – an interlocking set of geopolitical and corporate strategies, institutions, norms, behaviour patterns and policies that has created a space for the private car to flourish as the pre-eminent, and highly ineffective, global strategy of choice for mobility.[1] In short, we can call this car culture. This system works so well because it grew organically and now resides largely invisibly in the way global society operates. We have to break into this invisible façade to see what's going on. One of the reasons it is so difficult to do this and even talk about 'cities without the car' is because it is still largely useful, or at least perceived to be so, to humans in the course of their complicated daily lives. Cars still offer some level of comfort, convenience, speed and cost savings compared to other more sustainable mobility options such as mass rapid public transport, cycling and walking. And this will continue to be the case while the alternatives are impoverished and infantilised. They are being held back by the car culture complex. Arguments that keep us locked into car culture don't hold up to scrutiny and these need to be challenged, if the actual potential of other mobility options are to be unleashed.

The Carfree Cities movement states the problem thus:

The industrialized nations made a terrible mistake when they turned to the automobile as an instrument of improved urban mobility. The car brought with it major unanticipated consequences for urban life and has become a serious cause of environmental, social, and aesthetic problems in cities.[2]

Let's have a look at some of these threads of how we got into this mess.

The Geopolitics of Car Culture

In spite of all its limitations, the modern era has provided unrivalled mobility opportunities. People can relatively effortlessly and cost effectively move around cities, drawing largely on a temporary bonanza of abundant and cheap fossil fuel resources. This is a recent phenomenon. In the USA, where it largely all started, in 1900, there were only 8,000 motorised vehicles, and only 50 years later there were roughly 50 million.[3] By 2010, the number of motorised vehicles on our planet passed 1 billion and is likely to increase to 2 billion by 2035.[4] Annual global production stood at over 90 million units in 2017, a figure that has grown by 20 million over the last ten years. But it is the emerging economies such as Brazil, China, India and South Africa, which are set for really high levels of growth in car production and ownership in the years to come. In particular, China now produces and sells a staggering 30 million units per year.[5] Even in the UK, there are 25 million cars, a figure that is rising at 600,000 per year.[6]

Addiction to the car fuelled post-war economic expansion. One of its central pillars was a stable model of production, with the mass motor car industry and its car factory workers playing a central role. In 1907, 45,000 cars were produced in the USA, and by 1935, the figure was nearly 4 million. Henry Ford led the way, and his introduction of the assembly line in 1913 meant that he could produce thousands of his Model T every day.[7] This move was so important it went on to describe the industrial process underpinning post-war growth – Fordism. Through this, a virtual spiral of growth was instigated involving high output, high wages and high consumption. From these origins in the USA, car culture is now deeply ingrained in the DNA of the world's economy. China now accounts for the lion's share of global vehicle manufacturing production followed by the USA.[8] Eight million people are directly employed in making vehicles with another 50 million earning their living in associated trades. That's over 10 per cent of the world's total of manufacturing jobs.[9]

With growing levels of pollution and gridlock, many commentators are suggesting we may be reaching global 'peak car' – where annual global sales peaks as demand reduces.[10] But given the aggressive expansion plans of most large manufacturers, the continued expansion of middle-class consumers in the global South and their demand for mobility, and with the onset of driverless and semi-automated vehicles, it is unlikely that this onward trajectory of cars will abate. More and more cars seem set to pour off the production line and into our cities at exactly the time we need to moving in the opposite direction.

Car culture has been one of the global success stories for corporate control. The top five manufacturers, Toyota, General Motors, Volkswagen, Hyundai and Ford, account for over half of all production. Ford, General Motors and Chevron are all in the top 20 of the Fortune 500 list.[11] But the sphere of influence of corporate giants backing car culture needs to be widened to include the vast oil producers such as ExxonMobil, construction firms such as Balfour Beatty as well as new entrants like Google and Tesla who are cornering the driverless car market. The corporate world extracts profits from across the complex economy of car culture: its oil, roads, cars, credit, car parks and maintenance contracts. Locking down car culture, then, is not just about taking on auto-manufacturers but also a whole constellation of sectors which feed this fossil fuel behemoth. Moreover, the sheer amount of public subsidies that go into maintaining car culture is staggering. For example, in 2007, the European Environment Agency identified subsidies to transport worth €290 million a year, nearly half of which was taken by investments in road infrastructure.[12]

This wider story of car culture also brings us to the geopolitics of oil and war. Oil is a precious finite resource but it is mainly channelled towards car use. For example, around half of all oil consumed in the EU goes on road transport,[13] while in the USA, one-third of all energy consumed is used for transportation.[14] As neighbourhoods, economies and mobility patterns became locked into fossil fuel dependent transport across cities in the global North, nations needed to directly control the global oil production underpinning it. Given that easy and cheap supplies of oil have become scarcer over the twentieth century, global car culture has necessitated the control of oil reserves across the world, especially in the Middle East. The rise of a more independently minded OPEC[15] has meant that control of oil in the minority world needed to be secured through more militarised routes. Equally, as the easy oil has gone, more risky and damaging areas of exploration have been opened up to keep the oil supplies high. Tar sands, shale oils and pipelines through pristine wilderness areas all lead back to our roads. Car culture is a modern-day lesson in the geopolitics of corporate monopolies, militarisation and climate breakdown.

Welcome to the Global Car Park

Look around an urban area and most have a taken-for-granted look, function and feel. Street patterns, car parks, highways, transit systems all seem cast in stone – or at least concrete and steel. But it has not always been this way. The conversion of the city into a car-city has a relatively recent history. The modern combustion engine car as we know it emerged from France and Germany in the 1880s and only the first years of the twentieth century saw the emergence of the mass-produced car.

The early twentieth century represented a perfect storm, which facilitated the emergence and dominance of the motor car across the global North. Industrialisation and urbanisation connected and unfolded apace at a more global level, enhanced by an effective post-war industrial culture – super-charged by the militarisation of the global economy – and a renewed faith in modernist, large-scale planning. Other competing mobility options around railways, street cars, cable cars, buses, subways, rapid mass transport, walking, cycling and even the use of animals that could have flourished were dis-incentivised and locked out. For example, electric street cars spread across many North American cities in the early twentieth century. But suffering from underinvestment in the 1930s, some were bought by emerging car manufacturers and their subsidiaries, leading to conversions into fossil fuel powered buses throughout the 1950s.[16] Ironically, many cities are now returning to electric trams, streetcars and trolley buses after their 50-year flirtation with diesel buses. This is a significant side story as many of these early mass transit systems provided potential templates for how genuinely sustainable forms of urban mobility could unfold. In the second half of the twentieth century, cities were fundamentally remodelled through their lock into fossil-based motorised transport. Widespread advertising, government grants and federal subsidies, a realigned planning system and easy credit all facilitated this. Huge changes rolled out in the location of employment and residential areas, the nature of retail, the structure of the economy and the movement of goods. Vast suburbs for workers were facilitated by the advent of mass car transport, large national subsidies for road building, the growth of central employment districts and a con-sumer-based urban society.[17] Even in today's post-industrial, digitally enabled city this trend continues.

This modernist project of the motor car has now been exported into a global blueprint for urban development. The connection between prosperity, modernism and car culture is inscribed into the urban global psyche. To align urban space to the project of facilitating the private car has become the perverse task of the twentieth-century city. To be against car culture is to be anti-modern, anti-development, anti-jobs and anti-growth. In the upside down world we live in, to a certain extent, this is correct. The car-free city requires a fundamental rethink of our economic, residential, retail and planning system and a radical departure from the post-war model predicated on infinite economic growth. Car culture therefore, is one of the key drivers pushing the finite global biosphere towards its limits. We will return to this in other chapters.

The contemporary city is a vast car-processing machine. Cars have encouraged the further growth of a particular model of highly zoned city growth based around central business areas fed by arterial highways and linked to residential suburban neighbourhoods. Clearly, there was no international, national or even local agreements that laid down this car-city blueprint that permitted cars to take over city planning; but that is exactly what has happened. At times, it feels like the communities we live in and the street life that we depend upon is an inconvenience to getting as many cars around as fast as possible.

Urban areas are literally being taken over by car-based streetscapes. While dense European cities like Barcelona devote about 25 per cent of their space to streets, in places like Houston and Dallas, it is over 60 per cent.[18] Otherwise useful central city areas that could be parks, houses or workplaces have become huge temporary warehouses for cars, as people engage in their daily commute and park up 1,500 kilograms and £20,000 of metal for half of the day. They then struggle home through congested roads and park it as near to their house as possible for the other half. This is an impossibly irrational use of resources. City space is incredibly poorly allocated. So much precious land is tied up providing capacity for parking and short-term peak hour traffic flows. The sheer waste of human time of this lock-in is felt everywhere. A study conducted by the Dutch GPS seller TomTom found that commuters in Los Angeles spend 90 hours a year stuck in traffic.[19] Meanwhile, a study in the UK by ParkatmyHouse, a company that connects drivers with people who have available parking spaces, found that drivers spend 106 days of their lives looking for parking spots.[20]

The World Carfree Network put it thus:

> automobiles shape and distort our urban environment. They replace lively, pleasant, walkable, human-scaled communities with low-density, sprawled-out environments designed for getting elsewhere as fast as possible. With wide streets devoted to car traffic and vast seas of asphalt devoted to parking, our daily destinations are placed increasingly out of reach of our feet. Space for social interaction and cultural exchange is diluted and dispersed, inhibiting the informal social contacts that bind societies together. Life is pushed indoors, separated and compartmentalised.[21]

Faith is being placed on new technologies, semi-automated and driverless cars that can cut pollution and road deaths and create an efficient, rational transport utopia. But cities full with driverless cars will not stop the descent into alienated street life, status anxiety and debt-fuelled, corporate-controlled consumerism. The driverless car city is the next step of the great car takeover of the urban world.

Killer Cars

Now we come to the health impacts of car culture. A basket of problems are brought by the motor car: air pollution, noise, climate change costs, nature and landscape loss, and water and soil pollution. They are responsible for half of our air pollution, which is now a global public health crisis. While there are a number of other causes including coal, wood and waste burning, car culture, especially from diesel vehicles, is towards the top of the list.

After many European and North American countries thought they had dealt effectively with air pollution through Clean Air legislation and the reduction of pollution sources such as coal-based electricity generation, it has returned as an invisible killer. Outdoor air pollution is responsible for 3 million premature deaths a year worldwide.[22] Air pollution is now one of the main causes of premature death in the UK, second only to smoking. The UK Government's Committee on the Medical Effects of Air Pollutants concluded that 40,000 deaths a year can be attributed to air pollution.[23] And in China, it is estimated to account for around 17 per cent of all deaths.[24]

Transport contributes to this air pollution through the toxic gases NOx (all nitrogen oxides) and small particulate matter (pm) called PM2.5, which are linked with chronic bronchitis, lung cancer, heart disease, dementia and making conditions such as asthma worse. The presence of these gases and particulates is creating dangerous pollution hotspots in cities. The World Health Organization's air quality guideline suggests a PM2.5 annual limit of 10 micrograms per cubic metre (mpcm).[25] The shocking reality is that more than 80 per cent of people living in urban areas that monitor air pollution are exposed to air quality levels that exceed these limits.[26] In the UK alone, 44 urban areas, out of a total of 55, exceed it.[27] While all regions of the world are affected, populations in low-income cities are the most impacted. Currently, Delhi ranks as the world's worst urban area for air pollution. In late 2017, concentrations of PM2.5 reached just over 700, which is over double the mark of 300 that authorities deem as hazardous and may cause respiratory illnesses from prolonged exposure.[28] For millions of urban residents, simply living near a major highway is now a major public health risk.

The huge shift to diesel as a main fuel for new private cars and commercial vehicles, due to its comparative affordability and environmental credentials as a lower carbon emitter, is one of the key drivers. For example, the amount of nitrogen dioxide emitted by most diesel cars on roads in the EU is five times higher than legislation limits allow. It doesn't stop there. Diesel engines generate polycyclic aromatic hydrocarbons (PAHs), which are directly linked to mental health problems. PAHs exceed the WHO limit for 90 per cent of the EU urban population. As Robin Russell-Jones, the founder of the educational charity Help Rescue the Planet, notes, the extent to which car manufactures have been allowed to damage public health in Europe is scandalous.[29] The quickest and most effective way of reducing the damaging effects of diesel emissions is to rapidly bring forward the banning of diesel cars from central cities. Paris, Madrid, Athens and Mexico City have shown insight by announcing plans to ban diesel vehicles by 2025. But even this is years away. And we can anticipate a growing number of legal challenges against those slow to respond. For example, a successful court case has already been brought forward by Client Earth, a not-for-profit environmental law organisation, to ensure the UK government achieves compliance with EU legal limits for nitrogen dioxide emissions.[30]

As air pollution limits continue to be exceeded in cities across the world, there is a global failure of urban and public policy. Many cities have introduced clean air zones (CAZ) and low emission zones (LEZ) to tackle urban air pollution. But in most cases they are so unambitious that they are ineffective, mainly due to their very narrow coverage of land and vehicle types. Recent scientific studies have revealed that these zones have had negligible effects on ambient air quality.[31] Rather than rapidly reducing vehicular use, they merely displace it elsewhere with little net effect on city-wide pollution levels.

The link between car culture and climate change is also alive and growing, but not part of any meaningful public debate. The transport sector is responsible for up to one-third of total CO_2 emissions, and they continue to rise. The conclusion is clear: unless we will unlock ourselves from fossil fuel based transport, our ability to keep levels of global warming within the thresholds set by the 2015 UN Paris Accord will be undermined. While the shift towards hybrid, ultra-low and zero-energy vehicles is to be welcomed, it is unlikely that they will be rapidly enough. At the moment, such cars are around 1 per cent of total sales in China and France for example. Although as an indication of what can be achieved, a quite staggering level of almost one-quarter has been reached in Norway.[32] While growth is set to rapidly accelerate, and indeed all new cars sold could be zero emission by 2040, this is not enough. It will leave millions of greenhouse gas emitting cars on the streets for a generation. And a shift to electric-based mobility is only half the battle. It has to go hand in hand with a shift in electricity production from brown fuel sources to green, renewable ones. The task then is multifaceted and complex. Unlocking the car-free city requires a shift to renewable urban energy production, changes in mobility patterns and reductions in the number of vehicles.

Then there are the visible and direct road deaths. The World Health Organization compiles chilling facts on the topic. Well over 1 million people worldwide die each year from road traffic crashes, more than 3,000 people every day – half of which are vulnerable road users: pedestrians and cyclists. It is the leading cause of death amongst young people aged 15–29 years.[33] Almost all of the world's fatalities on the roads occur in low- and middle-income countries, even though these countries have approximately half of the world's vehicles.[34] The WHO predict that road traffic could become the seventh leading cause of death by 2030. And for this reason, the 2030 United Nation's Sustainable Development Goals has set ambitious targets of halving the global number of deaths and injuries from road traffic crashes by 2020.[35] And while road traffic deaths have been decreasing in more prosperous countries, this simply reflects the abandonment of city streets as people retreat to moving around by car. And it's not just about actual deaths, but also the greater sense of fear and anxiety in and around busy roads, especially for the elderly, children, pedestrians and cyclists. Finally, poor quality urban planning, which privileges car use is clearly undermining efforts to promote healthier mobility options, which involve physical activity and active commuting, especially amongst school children. Living Streets has emerged in the UK in this context to campaign for a walking nation, free from congested roads and pollution, in order to reduce the risk of preventable illness and social isolation.[36]

Mobility Injustice

While cars may still offer some benefits, these are not equally distributed. The dominance of cars brings with it a whole range of built-in social inequalities. Researchers have recently been interested in the strong links between poverty, mobility and the ideas of transport disadvantage and mobility injustice.[37] Social exclusion is built into the way we design our transport systems. Car culture simply mirrors existing disadvantage. Poorer communities miss out on a whole host of benefits including access to nearby and affordable bus and transit systems, and exclusions to costly private motor vehicles. The way transport systems have become colonised by corporate entities, as well as land use planning and zoning, reinforces poverty and social disadvantage. It creates 'transport poor' communities. When the city's transport system is designed around the private motor car and expectations of constant and extensive mobility, inequality will simply result. Not all social groups are treated equally in terms of their mobility needs. Well-designed transport systems that are built around diverse needs are key to accessing life's essential activities around employment, education, health and social networks. These transport disadvantages are merely widened as car-based urban sprawl expands, especially in places such as Australia and North America. In the UK, the Equality Trust found that the richest 10 per cent receives £977 million in transport subsidy, while the poorest 10 per cent receives just £297 million.[38]

While there are enough cars globally, they are not equally distributed. The number of households without cars is steadily decreasing, and in parallel the number of multiple car (especially in the three or more category) householders increasing. Car penetration in high-income countries such as the USA is extremely high, with over 90 per cent of households owning a car. But if we take the lowest 20 per cent of incomes, only 60 per cent of households own a car.[39] There is also of course significant variation as to whether people live in highly dense metropolitan areas with diverse transport options or sprawling car dependent ones. As well as being locked out of multiple and affordable transport options, poorer groups are also locked out of decision-making. This begs the question: what would a people-designed transport system look like? Defining socially just transport has to take on the complex task of identifying the winners and losers across a whole host of areas including access to transport options, as well as proximity to pollution hotspots and even the impacts of car-based pollution on future generations.

As Clayton Lane, Chief Executive of the Institute for Transportation and Development Policy, highlights, mass rapid transit is key to building an equitable city. In Los Angeles, only one in ten people in the metro region live within 1 kilometre of rapid transit. In the metro regions of Madrid and Barcelona, it is nearly three-quarters of all people.[40] But one of the key issues is that the majority of cities are not adequately providing for the lower-income population that lives outside the city limits, especially those who have to travel long distances into central areas to undertake precarious work in the hospitality and service sectors. This problem is particularly acute in the global South. For example, in Jakarta, which has a metro region population of 28 million, most people outside this metro area are not served by any form of transit to the central area.

I am My Car

One of the questions that has preoccupied researchers is why do cars remain the preferred mobility option, even in the face of evidence that there are safer, more environmentally friendly, healthier and cheaper ways to travel?[41] There remains a clear disconnect between the evidence of what car culture is doing to individuals, communities and the planet and what people tell themselves about the cars in their own life. Most of us would agree on the negative impacts of cars but also insist that their own car is indispensable to their life, family or work.

We ignore the psychology of car culture at our peril. We have to understand car culture in its broader historical and social context to understand how we got so addicted to it. While the automobile and the wider car culture around it became central to our economies, and even global geopolitical strategies, it's also become central to our sense of self. The car has adopted a much broader meaning and significance than a lump of metal to get us from A to B. If we don't grasp this psychological lock into car culture, we will be less effective in trying to unlock the potential of the car-free city. So how did this happen?

Cars are far from functional entities that move people around. They are now deeply connected with our emotions, personal and collective psyches and social status. It is easy to see why the humble car is allotted such a significant cultural role. When it first emerged, the early motor car was the preserve of the rich and represented status, freedom and independence. They offered the promise, but not the reality, of adventure, social status and power. And unlike communal public transport, the car taps into the deep-seated human desire to create a private home. Cars become an extension of our living rooms where we can play our own music and customise it to reflect our personal tastes. Marketers and manufacturers caught onto this. These were the things mass consumers yearned for and they would happily buy into. It's no surprise then, that the automotive industry is one of the biggest spenders when it comes to advertising. In 2012, amongst the world's largest corporations General Motors and Ford were respectively ranked number two and number seven for spending on advertising.[42]

The psychological desire for speed and power, which the car offers, is also under-appreciated. Academics have pointed out that the car is an extension of the longer-standing desire for fast mobility and personal freedom.[43] Our quick moving hunter-gather predecessors may have given us a biological urge to move fast. Tapping into these desires, people transform themselves behind the steering wheel, and car manufacturers are constantly pandering to this by increasing technological gadgets, speed and performance. The barrier to moving away from car culture, then, is the fact that the private car can be a very exciting machine. The thrill of speed is a psychological stimulant.

We also ignore at our peril the role of a car as a status symbol, which is used to impress, dominate and even seduce. Cars have become a proxy for physical and sexual prowess. In marketing, they take on characteristics of being hot, sexy and erotic. People literally love their cars.

They become a representation of self-love that also reflects a lack of meaningful human contact. People derive a significant sense of worth from their motor car. Cars have become the quintessential symbol of progress and self-worth. Walking, taking the bus or cycling to work often gains the status of sympathy as though the person somehow has not been able to enjoy the benefits of an advanced society. And this is especially the case in emerging market economies. As I explore later, one of the challenges is to create less exciting cars and car-based streetscapes. This involves changes in advertising and marketing, technical performance and also infrastructure changes. Cars simply have to become slower, more expensive, less convenient and more boring! But there also has to be a broader shift in our perceptions of ourselves as citizens in an inter-dependent web of relations rather than free-floating individuals able to act as they please. As I now explore below, to unlock the car-free city, the alternatives have to fill this gap. Those developing them not only have to make them feasible, practical and interesting, they also have to satisfy our human instincts.

UNLOCKING THE CAR-FREE CITY

The task is simple – we need to unlock cities from the car. This is a radical break with fossil fuel and individual-based transport. But my argument takes us far beyond the private car – it means decoupling urbanity from car culture. Eliminating cars from cities is really about eliminating the structural conditions that make cars necessary. What I have pointed to so far is a whole set of changes across advertising, manufacturing, economics, planning, infrastructure, leisure, consumerism, psychology and even geopolitics that need addressing.

There is also the pressing issue of necessity. To have a realistic chance of tackling the twin challenges of climate change and air pollution, car-free cities need to be the norm by the end of this century. Keeping to the kinds of strict global carbon budgets agreed at the UN Paris conference would mean an unprecedented increase in vehicle energy efficiency, mass shifts to other forms of mobility and alternative fuel sources. As we start the mammoth task of locking down fossil fuel based road transport, we need to unlock alternatives across all these areas on a mass scale to build momentum for the idea and the future reality of cities beyond cars.[44]

The good news is that this task is already underway. There are signs that in some more buoyant global North cities, the desire to own a car has been in decline for some time. This is particularly true amongst young digitally savvy millennials, who are moving away from car ownership towards car sharing and the use of public transit systems. And very high density cities like Tokyo and New York with excellent rapid transit systems show what can be achieved through coordinated state action, investment, the right incentives, pricing structures and a willing public culture. At 0.5 cars per household, car ownership in Tokyo is amongst the lowest in the world. The thorny issue is whether this retreat from the love affair with the car in selected cities can also spread to sprawling and rapidly expanding cities, especially in the global South.

The Car-Free Movement

The movement against the car is as old as the car itself. Significant opposition was evident to the 'horseless carriages' that emerged as the twentieth century dawned, which many saw as a dangerous and noisy menace to previously peaceful high streets. For example, Nantucket Island, south of Cape Cod, stood alone in the USA and successfully fought and held back to introduction of the automobile until 1918.[45] Throughout the twentieth century, early movements set the tone. Homes Not Roads in the 1970s highlighted the damaging effects of the expansion of major arterial routes on London communities, while Stop the City undertook blockades of the City of London to highlight profiteering and corporate greed. The UK went on to provide global inspiration through its anti-roads movement. After the Conservative Government launched the biggest road-building programme since the Romans, in 1989, a string of successful anti-road camps emerged from Twyford Down, the M11 link Road and the Newbury Bypass. In 1996, the year which marked 100 years of the car, road spending in the UK was slashed by £4 billion.[46] Seventy-seven planned roads were withdrawn. The movement against cars took a creative and dramatic turn throughout the 1990s, with Reclaim the Streets. From humble origins of small clusters of activists in London and San Francisco shutting down busy intersections, it grew into a global movement, replacing traffic with Situationist inspired street carnivals in places as diverse as Cape Town and Moscow.[47] In parallel, Critical Mass monthly protest cycle rides started in San Francisco in 1992, and ten years later the event was being held in over 300 cities around the world. These movements were successful in politicising a whole generation about the links between car culture, corporate globalisation, climate change and the lack of democratic control of urban space.[48] Given the continued pace of road building, we urgently need a resurgence of such movements.

Over the last few decades, a global car-free movement has now grown into an identifiable network encompassing social activists, urban planners, policy makers and campaign groups. They are brought together by a shared belief that motorised vehicles are now too dominant in cities and that action is being taken that can turn the tide away from cars. The World Carfree Network has become the legitimate voice for the global car-free movement. Growing out of the Car Busters movement, it is now an international network with a charter, steering committee, and almost 100 member organisations worldwide that coordinates global car-free actions and annual car-free city conferences. Its overall aim is to ultimately eliminate motorised vehicles, convert road space to public uses and rebuild compact urban environments based on walking, cycling or public transport.[49]

The Car-Free movement has built momentum through car-free days. Their aim is simple: to have a small amount of time in a city where cars are prohibited. One of the best known examples is in Bogota, which has seen private car ownership rise by three-quarters over the last decade, 600,000 children under five treated for breathing-related problems every year, 322 pedestrians and 56 cyclists killed in car-related accidents, and drivers losing an average of 22 days from traffic queues. Stroll out onto the busy streets of Bogota, Colombia's sprawling capital and you might expect to be choked by fumes, or forced into battle with vehicles weaving along a congested highway. Six days of the week, this is largely true. However, take a stroll on any Sunday and you encounter something entirely different – the Ciclovía. Translated as cycle route, over 120 kilometres of the city's roads are closed to cars and freely used in a range of other ways; rollerskating, cycling or walking with family and friends in an almost entirely car-free environment. First trialled in the 1970s, it was the pioneering imagination of former parks commissioner and his desire to give space usually dominated by cars back to ordinary Bogotános. The Ciclovía is a success with such a wide range of people as it is an opportunity for sports, meeting people, destressing and getting out into the fresh air. It also features the Recreovía, 28 stages across the city that are host to free classes in activities like rumba and aerobics.[50] Ciclovía has acted as a catalyst for change in many global cities; it allows citizens to reimagine their cities as places to live, work and play without the dominance of private traffic. It is these experiments that unlock collective imaginations around the way that urban space is managed, used and transformed by the people that inhabit them.

City car-free days have spread rapidly since. Early events in the 1990s in the European cities of Bath, Reykjavik and La Rochelle provided focus for what became a global and annual event in 2000 with the introduction of Global Care Free Day every 22 September. For one day, places as diverse as Paris' Champs-Élysées, Detroit's eight-lane Michigan Avenue and Calle de Alcalá, Madrid's longest street, are closed to traffic. Small and mega cities alike have joined this movement. Every Sunday morning, large parts of central Jakarta are closed to traffic, which results in 100,000 Jakartans gathering in the otherwise car-filled streets.[51] Chengdu, a lesser-known megacity of 10 million people in western China, now counts amongst World Carfree Day cities along with over 100 other Chinese cities.

Raahgiri Day is India's unique take on this global movement. First started in Gurgaon in 2010, India's fast growing and relatively prosperous Millennium city of around 1 million near New Delhi, Raahgiri is a word that connects with Mahatma Gandhi and brings together the ideas of journey and non-violence. It has now become a weekly event that closes city streets on Sunday mornings to cars to celebrate walking, biking, music-making and socialising.[52] It has also expanded to other Indian cities – most prominently to Dehli – bringing the world's second largest urban area into the car-free movement. Making cities genuinely car free will mean pushing these events beyond narrow non-business weekend mornings in central areas. But it is a start to bring the reality of car-free spaces into the contemporary DNA of city life.

Clearly, there is much more to be done and change won't come easy. Unravelling the car industrial–political–cultural complex won't happen overnight. And given the corporate might underpinning it, it might not happen at all. Creative, persistent and often risky action will be needed. Change won't come only from infrastructure changes, more enlightened land use planning or from cleverly pitching arguments around road deaths and climate change. The culture of cars has deep roots and needs weeding out of the contemporary social psyche using many tools. In the end, it is a question of a new urban politics. There will have to be moments of civil disobedience to support and super-charge the pace of change. Given the widespread and taken-for-granted nature of car adver-tising, subverting the messages of car culture will be key. Groups all over the world are undertaking billboard modifications to subvert corporate messages. This is a simple, if not entirely legal, way to reclaim the urban realm and intervene in the saturation of advertising in public space. As well as locking down car advertising, we need to unlock the potential of advertising to make sustainable mobility options cool. The company Buzzbike has an interesting take on this dilemma. They provide free use of a bicycle to London cyclists in exchange for the right to use the bike as a moving advertising platform, complete with Bluetooth connectivity that offers passers-by discounts.

Reclaim the City

Cities across the world have woken up to the scale of the crisis. Some have led the way to show what is possible. Thousands have introduced city bike and car-pool schemes offering low-cost alternatives to the private car. In particular, the Chinese-based bike sharing company Ofo is slowly spreading across the world, and now operates in over 250 cities. Congestion charging and clean air zones are spreading too, to disincentivise and prohibit higher polluting diesel vehicles from central areas. Other measures include temporarily suspending traffic when air pollution reaches dangerous limits, car sharing and changes to planning to reduce car use. Landmark examples came from Scandinavia. In Denmark, cycling policies were adopted as a direct consequence of the 1973 oil crisis, and bike advocacy in the Netherlands began through campaigns against traffic deaths called 'stop child murder'. Today both countries have high modal shares of cycling, despite high car ownership rates.[53]

The Danish capital, Copenhagen, is the most globally well-known city for its bicycle infrastructure. The number of bikes has now exceeded that of cars: 265,700 of the former compared with 252,600 of the latter.[54] Most other cities recoil with horror at the prospect of getting anywhere close. But as Klaus Bondam, head of the Danish Cycling Federation, points out it is ultimately replicable: 'It is not in our genes, it's not in our water. What we've shown the rest of the world is that if you build protected infrastructure, people will start riding their bikes.'[55] It is clear that policy makers in Denmark were ahead of the game in identifying the myriad problems associated with the over-dominance of private cars in their cities. Rather than simply prohibiting them and dealing with the knock-on effects, alternatives were put in place. Heavy investments have been made into cycle and metro infrastructure and then car space has slowly been taken away.

Those facing the largest challenges have often led the way. Cities panicked by the health effects of transport pollution, such as Paris, Delhi and Mexico City, have been more forceful and begun to ration access. New York, under its visionary transport commissioner, Janette Sadik-Khan between 2007 and 2013 transformed New York with 400 miles of cycling routes, a bike-share scheme and remodelled Times Square.[56] Over 140 acres of street space was taken from cars and reallocated to pedestrians and bikes. It has long been a preoccupation of European cities to tame the motor car and preserve active and dense street life that is seen as the keystone of civilised urban life. Venice, for obvious reasons, is probably the most car-free city in the world, followed closely by the likes of Hamburg, Helsinki, Milan and Copenhagen. Streetscapes continue to be re-engineered in ways that reverse the trends of the latter half of the twentieth century. The pioneering architect Jan Gehl has persuaded scores of cities to remodel central areas to force more space for people in the crucial area he calls 'life between buildings'.[57] Barcelona is tackling this in exciting new ways by freeing up vast swathes of roads currently used by cars in the Eixample neighbourhood, creating a number of superilles (superblocks), where car flows are restricted to residents at 10kmph, in what are dubbed as citizen spaces.

Moreover, after years of pushing highways into central areas, around the world there are the beginnings of a motorway–city reversal. In Madrid, 24 of the city's busiest streets are planned for redesign for walking instead of cars. Major roads are being torn down and reconstructed into new public spaces including: the M-30 ring road in Madrid, which was removed to create the Madrid Rio green space; the removal of the Embarcadero Freeway in San Francisco and the Park East freeway in Milwaukee; and the removal of a highway in Seoul to create a five-mile long recreation area called Cheonggyecheon.[58] Interestingly, Leeds in the north of England where I live and write this book appears in Wikipedia as one of the leading examples of car-free cities due to a 400m² patch of the city centre that has been entirely pedestrianised.[59] This little-known and refreshingly progressive fact is muted somewhat by the collar of cars that surrounds the city centre. Moreover, as new cities emerge, especially in the fast growing global South, efforts are being taken not to repeat the mistakes of the past and design out the car. For example, Great City, a new satellite city planned in Southwest China could serve as a model for a modern suburb. Instead of a layout that makes it necessary to drive, the streets are designed so any location can be reached in 15 minutes on foot.

It is also going to take creative citizen action to further open up the car-free city. Park(ing) is one example – an incremental, open-source urban tactic that reclaims street space from parked cars – which has its roots in San Francisco. In 2005, its proponents were frustrated with the pervasive and unequal distribution of street space in the city in favour of private cars. The art and design studio Rebar decided to take advantage of legal loopholes in the city's administrative system, legitimately paying for a car parking space for a few hours and setting up a temporary park in place of a vehicle. The initial pilot project transformed a section of the road from one dedicated to storing cars to one that existed for people to sit, socialise or relax in. In the face of a perpetually dominant car presence in our cities, this straightforward idea has struck a chord with citizens across the globe. Park(ing) day has now become an annual worldwide event every September across over 150 cities.[60] Moreover, Playing Out emerged in 2007 in Bristol through discussions between parents who were frustrated about their children's lack of freedom to play outside, mainly due to the dangers posed by cars. They used existing processes for closing roads for street parties to create a temporary car-free play space for the children in their local area. The idea has spread and Bristol City Council has now created the Temporary Play Street Order, which enables residents to close a street to traffic. Now over 100 streets across 30 cities in the UK are 'playing out' on a regular basis.[61]

These examples are beginning to build the car-free city from the bottom up. But they are the low-hanging fruit. From these quick wins, a momentum for broader structural change needs to be built which begins to lock out the car permanently. The difficult reality is that there is no win–win situation – car culture, and its advocates, is too rapacious and petulant to be able to live alongside a sustainable future. Precious urban space taken up by roads needs reallocating on a huge scale, through national and international legislation. And as we can now see, some cities have been brave enough to do this. However, many city governments are facing negative public reaction, which is hampering their widespread uptake. Even in socially progressive Oslo, ambitious plans to create a completely car-free city centre were retrenched due to oppositions from residents. They have now gone for a more gradual approach around a car-lite city centre encouraging changes through subsidies to cycles, removing car parking spaces and extending the pedestrian network.[62]

Rethinking Mobility After the Age of the Car

Our desire for instant and faster forms of mobility has remained unquestioned and unchecked. If we are to set a new course for genuine urban sustainability, we simply have to moderate our desires for mobility. The very need for such intense mobility needs to be questioned. Transport is normally bunched into peak hours in the morning and afternoon. These peaks can be shifted, but they would require quite complex behavioural and organisational adjustments. Large city employers in health, government and education can stagger their starting and ending times to spread the load. This would go hand in hand with the reduction and distribution of working hours. Major arterial routes in and out of cities are particular sticking points. They need to be rethought as veins and arteries taking one-way flows of sustainable mobility options in and out of cities.

Rethinking mobility options goes hand in hand with rethinking planning and zoning, and eroding the need for mass, wasteful commuting from neighbourhood to central work zones. Central areas need to be replanned, with work more broadly distributed throughout neighbourhood centres. Food and retail needs rescaling and decoupling from car use. Freiburg in Germany is one of the most instructive examples of what can be achieved. It has achieved a three-way equal split of journeys between cars, cycling and walking. Its neighbourhood of Vauban has been designed almost entirely car free with a staggering three-quarters of journeys taken by bike. And there are real, tangible health benefits from active commuting. A study conducted by UK Biobank and supported by the Department of Health in the UK, involving over half a million adults found that active commuting (compared with passive commuting by car or bus), particularly with a cycling component was associated with a lower risk of adverse health outcomes, including cardiovascular disease, diabetes and some cancers.[63] These findings are a call to action: a huge conversion of people cycling and walking to work, leisure or retail options would save a substantial number of lives and significantly reduce national health budgets.

Unlocking the car-free city directly means powering up flexible, sustainable and multimodal mobility systems. Helsinki is pioneering the way here with plans it calls 'mobility on demand'. Behind this is Mobility as a Service (MaaS), a technologically driven Finnish mobility company that seeks to reshape global transportation markets. MaaS essentially acts as an operator between service users and providers, combining all existing transport services, including public transport, taxis, ferries, shared bikes and rental cars into a single mobile app on the 'single-ticket principle' so citizens can create personalised transport plans. It is driven by a sub-scription service that acts as a journey planner and payment platform and makes multi-modal journeys easier to navigate. It has already been shown to improve traffic flow and the overall environmental impacts of transport.[64]

In the short term, we have to use cars in a smarter way. Given changes in the wider economy, the whole status of the car is being rethought anyway. In the sharing economy, it no longer makes sense to privately own a car – to personally invest in a vast amount of expensive metals, plastics and electrical componentry. As the desire to buy a new car outright declines, new methods of ownership and use around pooling and sharing are emerging. Smart technologies are promoting novel ways of locating, renting and leasing cars in cities. As well as leading in cycling and rail infrastructure, Denmark is also host to the most mature car-sharing market in the world. DriveNow, operated by Arriva and Sixt, was recently launched in Copenhagen based around a car fleet of 400 BMWs and Minis. Green Mobility, also owned by Sixt, has a fleet of 450 electric cars across Copenhagen. Between them, they have the largest fleet of electric cars in the world. These are part of the city's mature car-sharing platforms, including LetsGo, GoMore and Moveabout. We need to see ourselves as temporary users of cars that ultimately need to be rationally shared around the city in combination with other mobility options. And while semi-automated vehicles won't do much to tackle car culture, they do, in the medium term, offer the potential for encouraging collective ownership, peer-to-peer use and rational resource sharing.

Mass rapid transit is key to shifting away from the car. But each word here needs attention: it has to be accessible for everyone especially in terms of cost; it has to be quicker than other options; and it has to go everywhere. The southern Brazilian city of Curitiba is one of the landmark cases. With 2 million residents, this city established the first and now one of the biggest lowest cost bus systems in the world – the Bus Rapid Transit (BRT). Opened in the 1970s under visionary mayor Jaime Lerner, around 70 per cent of the population use it. Users pay a flat fee, queue in raised plastic pods making the boarding process efficient, and the buses travel on dedicated lanes. It is based on a genuine integrated network allowing users to travel throughout the city. Now mass transit systems have spread to 186 cities across the world. And there are so many other glimpses of radical change. Shenzhen, China, has the largest zero-emissions fleet worldwide with more than 6,000 vehicles – and aiming to get to 35,000 in the next few years. Rio de Janeiro has built 150km of new bus rapid transit infrastructure, increasing the percentage of population using mass transit from 18 per cent in 2009 to 63 per cent in 2016. It is also building 450km of bike lanes to further reduce automobile use.[65]

Given that cars won't disappear anytime soon, a priority action area remains simply slowing them down and constraining their use – with the aim of making roads safer. As the World Health Organization reminds us, an adult pedestrian's risk of dying is less than 20 per cent if struck by a car at 50kmph (30mph) and almost 60 per cent if hit at 80kmph (50mph). Speed restricted home zones have become a widespread tool for taming the car, where streets are redesigned to facilitate the safe coexistence of different modes of transport, restricting the ability of vehicles to drive in a straight line for any significant distance. There is a wonderful diversity of such initiatives such as home zones in the UK, woonerf in the Netherlands (literally, living streets), zones de rencontre in France and calles residenciales in Spain. In these zones, pedestrians are seven times less likely to be fatally injured if hit by a car compared to higher speeds of 50kmph (30mph). There are also increasing moves to designate speed limits across extensive areas of cities. In 2016, Edinburgh designating 80 per cent of all its streets with a 20mph limit, with a similar amount in the cities of Bristol and Brighton, and several London boroughs introducing widespread 20mph speed limits in the last few years. Vision Zero in Sweden, sets the tone. Enshrined in Swedish law, it establishes an ultimate target of no deaths or serious injuries on Sweden's roads and is not satisfied with merely reducing accidents to an economically manageable level. While these kinds of efforts do not guarantee success, they do begin to lay out clear parameters for safer and shared mobility options.

*   *   *

Putting ourselves front and centre of unlocking potential is one of the most crucial but difficult tasks ahead. We are not stuck in traffic. We are the traffic. Recognising our own personal implication in car culture, and the damage it is doing, is personally threatening. So much is invested in it, that it is easier to ignore it. For many of us, perhaps the car represents the only crumb of sanity, freedom and control in an otherwise out of control world. It might be the only way we can get food, get our kids to school and get to work in a world full of complicated, expensive and seemingly dangerous options. But we need a step change. The leading transport advocate, John Whitelegg, has pointed to what might underpin a paradigm shift towards a sustainable and socially just urban transport system: moving away from considerations of time, savings and cost benefit analysis towards issues of climate change, social equality and sustainability as the drivers of planning decisions, a huge shift away from subsidies in transport linked to climate breakdown, a complete rethink about how we approach road safety, especially in terms of reductions in speed and zoning, and new forms of democratic participation.[66] This is the challenging agenda for unlocking the car-free city, and one that has to be urgently grasped.

2

The Post-Carbon City

Our urban lives are built and dependent on huge energy throughputs. More worryingly, contemporary urbanity is saturated in finite, polluting and climate-changing fossil fuel energy resources.[1] The staggering and rapid growth of cities over the post-war period has been lock stepped with access to a historically unprecedented fossil fuel bonanza of cheap coal, oil and gas. We see this in the movement of people, the construction and heating of buildings, the distribution of food, the expansion of leisure and retail, and the flow of goods and services. From this vast and cheap energy resource, we have built up complex cities capable of immense prosperity, but also of inequality. Using these precious energy resources, we have created cities of leisure and toil, luxury and squalor, beauty and ugliness, utility and folly.

But as Richard Heinberg, leading advocate of a post-oil world, has forcefully reminded us, this energy party is nearly over.[2] The plentiful energy resources that have allowed this great urban expansion of late modernity are fragile, fleeting as well as deeply damaging and unequally distributed. In the absence of a stable and safe energy resource to underpin city life, how urban energy needs will be met in the decades to come is a sobering and fearful prospect. Of course, cities flourished before the age of fossil fuels, and many city dwellers around the world have never enjoyed its current benefits. Vast urban growth continues on the edge of cities with little access to energy resources. These examples are instructive about the possibilities for urban life beyond fossil fuels. But a new urban energy deal is urgently required, if we are to tackle the challenges of climate breakdown, resource scarcity, social injustice and ensure a good level of development for a growing human population. Considering that in the coming years, an estimated three-quarters of humanity will live in cities, accounting for 80 per cent of total energy demand and 70 per cent of global emissions,[3] the need for cities to unlock themselves from fossil fuels is paramount.

This is the post-carbon city challenge. I use this as provocative shorthand for exploring what urgently needs to come next, after the profligate fossil fuel era. Large parts of city life are locked into an ageing centralised, corporate controlled and externally dependent energy system unfit for the challenges ahead. Through their buildings, leisure, tourist and retail habits, transport, workplaces, producer and consumer services, cities continue to be vast non-renewable energy users. Current city energy systems lock citizens into an energy commodity that is priced for the benefit of concentrating wealth and global political power rather than creating a common good that underpins a flourishing life for all. The negative results are all around us: localised pollution, increases in greenhouse gas (GHG) emissions, fuel poverty and high utility prices. The post-carbon city lays down an energy challenge that is far from just a technical or infrastructure one. As I explore below, it requires widespread cultural, policy, political, economic and organisational change and the creation, provision and use of energy based around a very different set of values, especially energy justice.

The aim of this chapter is not to rehearse the technical details of power sources, fuel mixes or the practicalities of energy infrastructures in the city. As I hope is clear by now, this book is rather different. Instead, I explore those cities and innovators who have embarked upon a journey to unlock their localities from rapidly depleting and unsustainable fossil fuel sources of the urban carbon age and realize the potential of what I call the post-carbon city. The task is clear. Mitigating the effects of climate breakdown as far as possible is now a global priority. Extreme weather events are disrupting city life. Air pollution levels are slowly poisoning urban dwellers. Concerns over unstable energy supplies and corporate oligopolies are mounting. In this context, a civic energy revolution is spreading fast. Attention is rapidly focusing on the shift away from fossil fuel supplies. The energy industry is in transition, innovation is spreading fast and renewable energy options cost less than ever before. Before we turn to this great post-carbon unlocking, let's have a closer look at the carbon age.

THE CARBON AGE

The post-carbon city is not to be taken literally. It doesn't mean a world without carbon – one of the building blocks of our world. It is shorthand for the urgent action required in the face of global carbon budgets that are being pushed beyond safe limits due to the introduction of high levels of human induced GHGs. These have been increasing rapidly since the Industrial Revolution through deforestation and the continued use of hydrocarbon fossil fuels. The post-carbon city is an agenda where carbon-emitting activities are deployed more responsibly and equitably, and ultimately phased out, by our economies and societies. Indeed, a route to a less carbon dependent world will require, along the way, carbon intensive industries to manufacture new homes, production processes and renewable technologies, as well as equitable carbon allowances for poorer countries.

There is a clear agenda for urgent change which is pushing cities in this direction. It has taken many decades, but now there is international recognition of the scale and nature of the task ahead. How to reduce the ecological footprint of humanity is essential given that we are exceeding the carrying capacity of the global biosphere in terms of GHG emissions. In 2013, the Intergovernmental Panel on Climate Change (IPCC) laid down the scale of the challenge through global carbon budgets. Humanity can only emit between 800 billion and 1,200 billion more tonnes of carbon, if it wants to stay within safe limits of global tempera-ture increases. At a rate of 50 billion tonnes of carbon emissions per year, that leaves around 25 years, or one generation, for decisive action.[4]

What the scientific community states is that GHG emissions urgently need to be brought within safe limits of 350 parts per million (ppm) or lower, compared to the current level of over 400ppm and rising. Without a real breakthrough moment, current agreements are setting the globe on a course to levels of concentrations of 450ppm or above, and that this will take levels of global warming beyond the critical level of 2 degrees Celsius. Above this level, a whole host of interconnected threats unfold around, for example, biodiversity and habitat loss, food scarcity, loss of land, mass migrations, the spread of diseases, extreme weather patterns and sea-level rises.[5]

Emission reduction road maps are required which can reduce emissions by up to 100 per cent by 2050 (relative to 1990 baselines) to get us back near the 350ppm level and avoid dangerous levels of warming. In fact, there is a growing awareness that we need to go beyond this. The Australian think-tank, Beyond Zero Emissions, states that we need to get to levels more like those seen in pre-industrial times of around 280pm to stabilise the global biosphere. This will require a blanket moratorium on the use of all fossil fuels, a shift to 100 per cent renewable energy sources as well as a mass take-up of carbon sequestering activities.[6] The EU and the UK has started work in this direction with action plans that set a course towards 80 per cent reductions by 2050.[7] However, it's still unclear what needs to be done to generate even these lower reductions. Decarbonising our urban societies and economies is a huge task. It involves longer term and structural changes, which will fundamentally alter the form and function of the way we live our lives.

Clearly, the post-carbon city agenda is a fraught and fragile one. It is situated within the complex geopolitical story and vested interests that underpin our modern energy system. Concentration of ownership is a hallmark right across the energy chain from oil production to electricity generation and supply. Globally, the supply of oil is concentrated in the hands of large national country producers including, by far the biggest, Saudi Aramco, followed by Russia's Gazprom, the National Iranian Oil Company, PetroChina, Mexico's Pemex, interspersed with the traditional global giants of BP, Shell, ExxonMobil and Chevron. What goes with such concentrated ownership are the geopolitical struggles for power between nations and associated conflicts and wars. This picture may become even more volatile as global supplies diminish.

Taking a look at national energy markets, ownership is immensely concentrated. In the UK, for example, three companies account for the generation of all electricity, with the French-owned EDF accounting for one-quarter and the German-owned RWE accounting for over 10 per cent. Similarly, the 'big six' suppliers (British Gas, E.ON, EDF Energy, nPower, Scottish Energy and SSE) control over 90 per cent of supply to customers. Transmission and distribution are also largely in private hands through the National Grid.[8] In spite of the continued growth of renewables, most national systems are also still dependent on 'brown' rather than 'green' energy mixes. In the USA, fossil fuels and nuclear account for nearly 90 per cent of electricity generation,[9] and in the UK the figure is about 75 per cent.[10] These levels of concentration stifle renewable energy innovation and continue to lock energy infrastructures into maximising short-term gains for shareholders.

At a city level, piecing together accurate data on energy use is complex. Many goods and services used within city boundaries are generated from energy, and hence create emissions outside those boundaries. In fact, the more prosperous and connected the city, the greater this issue. This could underestimate a city's energy consumption and emissions by 50 per cent. But there are also some real global differences, as recent research led by a German and US team highlights.[11] In most developed economies, energy use and hence per capita emissions in cities are lower than their national average. This points to cleaner fuel mixes, especially lower carbon gas and electricity fuels and more efficient and effective urban infrastructures, as well as an affluence effect based around investment in low-carbon technologies. The opposite is the case in the global South where cities, especially mega cities, have energy and emission per capita higher than their national average. This highlights a reliance on dense and brown fuels especially oil and extensive polluting infrastructures in cities, as well as the sheer number of urban inhabitants, but also the still sizable non-urban populations. This same research found that a variety of approaches will be required to reduce energy consumption in cities of differing contexts. For example, given the likely continued urban expansion, particularly in Asia, promoting more compact and denser forms, functions and mobility patterns in global South cities as they grow could be one of the most fruitful intervention strategies to reduce planetary GHG emissions.

Significant political will and legislative action are needed to unravel the interconnected aspects of an urban energy system from their current high levels of concentration and dependency on fossil fuels. A theme I return to repeatedly is the real limits that exist to unlocking sustainable cities beyond a certain point. Attempts to establish post-carbon pathways often stall after the low-hanging fruit of easy building retrofits, shifts to hybrid vehicles and small technical adjustments; but a more fundamental decoupling of economic growth with carbon emissions is required. The concept of Factor 10 suggests that increases in productivity can go hand in hand with a tenfold reduction in impact and resource use, in order to avert climate breakdown and allow developing countries adequate resources to grow.[12] Making carbon reduction plans at this level within the economy is a fundamental challenge to the current pro-growth global economy and its established measures of GDP. Kevin Anderson of the Tyndall Centre for Climate Research has been one of the tireless advocates for radical emission reduction scenarios, if we are to keep within safe levels of GHG emissions. This involves not just so-called negative emission technologies, but also currently unpalatable contractions of economic activity, possibly in double digits. Current levels of economic growth, at say 1 or 2 per cent, require huge leaps of efficiency to offset the emissions embedded in them. But the problem is that even small levels of emission cuts are usually only experienced during times of economic recession. And embarking on emission cuts of towards 10 per cent evokes the kind of collapse experienced in post-Soviet Russia.[13] As I explore in Chapter 5, the challenge is to develop a steady state, or even de-growth, economic agenda into a palatable social deal that still ensures relative levels of prosperity.[14] What this means and how it would be implemented at a city level is poorly understood. The kinds of urban decarbonisation required would radically transform current social and economic relations beyond all recognition.

THE POST-CARBON CITY AGENDA

The Post Carbon Institute (PCI), a public think-tank based in the USA, leads the way in defining the post-carbon agenda. It defines it as responding 'to the interrelated economic, energy, environmental, and equity crises that define the twenty first century. We envision a world of resilient communities and re-localized economies that thrive within ecological bounds'.[15] Their work on the post-carbon agenda is necessarily broad and encompasses climate, consumption and waste, communities, culture and behaviour, ecology, economics, education, energy, food and agriculture, government, health, population, social justice, transportation and water. One of their research team, Daniel Lerch, brought an essential urban inflection to this debate. He outlined five principles to work towards a post-carbon city: dealing with transportation and land use; tackling private energy consumption; using multiple solutions at different scales; planning for fundamental changes; and building a sense of community. Taken together, these are a radical road map for cities of the future.[16]

The post-carbon agenda, then, operates at different levels of complexity. Given its associations with hydrocarbon fuels and carbon emissions, in its simplest form, the post-carbon agenda is generally associated with addressing the overuse of hydrocarbon fuels including oil, gas and coal, and ensuring energy descent pathways away from these, mainly to tackle climate breakdown. It also points towards the need for governance structures that are neither over-reliant on just the market nor the state which increases empowerment, local self-management, accountability and neighbourhood-level participation, especially in terms of the generation and supply of energy. Moreover, the high levels of hydrocarbon use directly underpin the 'business-as-usual' pro-growth economic model predicated on individualist and consumerist values and high resource throughputs. The wider challenge is how health, well-being and prosperity can be achieved without seriously undermining the social and ecological systems that urban areas rely upon.[17]

In the face of these challenges, some of the most innovative action is emerging at the city and neighbourhood level. A big driver here is the real lack of decisive national and international policy-making and action. But at the city level, innovation is not so restrained by the huge task of agreements between diverse interests, parties and nations. The constraints and lobbying of powerful nations is not as evident. On one level, the task in cities is clearer, especially if it is supported by visionary leadership that works across silos. Action aimed at decoupling activities from fossil fuels at a city scale will have immediate effects, given that cities consume about 75 per cent of global primary energy. City action is also deeply self-motivated, given that they are affected by the impacts of dependency on hydrocarbon activities ranging across air pollution from industry and automobiles, or the risk of coastal flooding from sea-level rises.

This combination of self-interest and innovative capacity is marking the way for decisive post-carbon city action. To tackle fossil fuel dependency and climate breakdown in cities requires novel and brave forms of governance, and we are only just beginning to see this. Drastic reductions in GHGs and energy use will only be achieved through developing a radically different and more collective sense of what it means to be a citizen, not mistaking this with being a consumer, and reworking how our economies work to underpin prosperity. If it is to address the seriousness of issues, the post-carbon agenda is no less a new socio-economic–ecological deal based on overcoming the limits of the carbon age through economic decarbonisation, de-growth and eventually a steady state economy (where resource inputs and outputs are balanced), a moratorium on fossil fuel use, a relocalisation of daily life, rapid action to regenerate natural systems and assets, and reclaiming space for greater popular control and common ownership from both the market and state.

Pathways to Zero-Carbon Cities

There is no one-size-fits-all approach for post-carbon cities. Each will have its own trajectory based on its unique combination of history, culture, politics and economics, as well as scale and role in the wider economy. Urban energy use is spread across a complex range of sectors and activities including industry, buildings (in terms of construction, heating and lighting), leisure, commerce, retail and mobility. The overall draw of energy across these sectors varies wildly between cities. Those experiencing rapid development booms will have expanding construction activities often fuelled by foreign inward investment, others will have energy intensive mobility patterns, or a legacy of older high-energy industries. For example, in Beijing, almost two-thirds of emissions come from industry, with one-third coming from buildings and only a small proportion coming from transport, while in Katmandu and Cape Town, it is roughly the opposite. Equally, some will be making concerted efforts to reinvent themselves as low-carbon cities and unlock city life from high levels of carbon emitting energy sources. And there are those who are yet to benefit from high levels of global North style development, fossil fuel energy systems or have been ravaged by war and conflict.[18]

Moving forward with energy and GHG reduction pathways, every city will need to focus on its sectors where energy consumption is locked in and focus on the areas of potential. Future urban energy pathways, then, will vary according to the starting point of each locality, its overall understanding of the challenge and crucially its capacity to act meaningfully. Some lower-income cities might be playing catch-up and be permitted to use extra resources especially to transition their infrastructure, while more energy bloated cities will need to detox quicker. Whatever pathways are chosen, careful consideration and mutual understanding will be needed to nurture broad agreement between sectors to minimise social conflict.

Footprinting analysis is a useful tool to get a sense of the scale of the task. It measures the amount of biologically productive land and water area a given territory uses to produce the resources it consumes and to absorb the waste it generates.[19] Cities have wildly varying footprints both in terms of their energy and ecological requirements. What we need to aim towards is restoring a balance between a city's actual geographical footprint and the footprint of material resources that it requires to sustain itself. This is often called one planet living.[20] Many North American cities, for example, have an ecological footprint 20 times that of many African cities. There is an important global justice issue here. While some cities feast on dense and cheap energy and natural resources, others face an energy famine. What is clear is that vast swathes of the world's urban poor have very little access to cheap energy compared to the bloated and energy dense lives of more affluent urban inhabitants. Equalising access to energy both between and within cities is a central issue, especially in terms of addressing poverty at a city, national and global level. And while we need to share the spoils of economic growth, we also need to contract energy use as we do so. The Contraction and Convergence model first developed by the Global Commons Institute in the 1990s is useful here. As an idea, it entails reducing overall global emissions of GHGs to a safe level (contraction), as a result of every country bringing its emissions per capita to a level, which is equal for all countries (convergence). Some countries, especially in the global South, may be able to continue to use energy in order to, for example, make a rapid shift to green energy and ensure good levels of development, while others have to reduce as long as the long-term plan is to converge around a lower point.[21]

Several route maps have been developed that can help cities transition towards lower-carbon and even zero-carbon energy systems. Early pioneering work into energy transitions has been undertaken by Richard Heinberg.[22] In this work, he made a convincing case for embarking on a global energy descent away from cheap fossil fuel energy to avoid the impacts of climate breakdown and the social conflicts likely to ensue with less readily available and affordable energy – what has become known as peak oil. While such peaking of oil scenarios have largely failed to materialise in the timescales predicted, in large part because of the commercial exploitation of new resources around liquid coal and tar sands, the basic premise holds: the cheap abundant supplies have gone and urban society still needs to wean itself away from finite and climate dangerous fossil fuel energy sources. More pressing, the global scientific community now agree that we cannot afford to burn more than two-thirds of the remaining fossil fuel reserves, if we want to avoid catastrophic levels of global warming within this century.

A number of detailed studies have emerged to show how to feasibly and successfully enact zero-carbon energy transitions. In the UK, the most comprehensive is the Zero Carbon Britain plan developed by the pioneering Centre for Alternative Technology. This plan outlined how it is technically feasible to embark upon a rapid decarbonisation scenario as a nation, where GHG emissions are reduced to net zero by 2030 through powering down to cut energy demand, and powering up by much greater use of renewables and existing technologies particularly offshore wind turbines, biomass and smart grids.[23] This plan is groundbreaking as it is not afraid to name and confront issues of energy over-consumption and energy equality. Most relevant, this zero-carbon framework is now being explored at the city level. In my own region, Zero Carbon Yorkshire has emerged as a mobilising idea to decarbonise activities across different sectors.

Similarly, Energy Descent Action Plans (EDAP) at the community level have also taken hold through the Transition Towns movement to help guide localities towards a more resilient future in the face of the peaking of oil supplies. While the early drama of peak oil thinking has subsided, it remains a powerful tool for localities to think through the crucial steps needed to move away from fossil fuel dependency, reduce GHG emissions and develop resilient economies. The first fully formed EDAP emerged in the English town of Totnes. Called Transition In Action, it was created by the local community and sees the changes necessitated by climate change, peak oil and financial austerity not as a crisis, but as a huge opportunity for enterprise, creativity, community, enhanced resilience and a greater quality of life.[24]

David Holmgren, a permaculture advocate and practitioner, has focused on the transition strategies needed for communities to adapt to the peaking of affordable oil supplies, climate breakdown and the associated social conflict. He outlines four possible scenarios, depending on how fast oil supplies decline, and how serious climate breakdown turns out to be: brown tech, where new supplies are used to maintain the status quo and some of the worst climate change scenarios unfold; green tech, where significant investment in renewable technology allows a degree of centrally planned strategic localisation; earth stewards, where oil shortages crash the global economy forcing a bottom-up rebuild of the economy; and lifeboats, what he calls the disaster scenario, where both climate change and resource decline are severe and society breaks down.[25] This kind of scenario planning is now extremely widespread. The key point to recognise about them is that they tend to reflect the inbuilt and largely invisible assumptions, ideologies and theories of change of their creators. Each scenario contains a labyrinth of financial, social, organisational, political and behavioural assumptions that need to be unpacked.

In addition, the Ecological Sequestration Trust was formed in 2011 to demonstrate at city-region scale how to create a step change in improving energy, water and food security in the face of the combined challenges of climate, demography and increasing resource-scarcity. It adopts a transformative approach based on three assumptions: that by

2030 GHG emissions need to be 50 per cent of 1990 levels; the global ecological footprint is brought back towards the carrying capacity of the biosphere that can sustain it; and that there is a focus on increasing the human development index rather than solely upon economic growth. It is trialling its approach in demonstrator projects as diverse as Accra and Mongolia through what they claim is the world's first open-source, integrated human–ecology–economics systems platform that enables resilient disaster risk sensitive planning, policy-making, investment and procurement for city-regions.[26]

The author and entrepreneur Jeremy Rifkin has gained significant global momentum for what he calls the Third Industrial Revolution (TIR). Rifkin explores how internet technology and renewable energy can work together to create what he calls lateral power – a new economic growth dynamic, where homes, offices and factories create their own green energy and share it with each other in an energy internet. This TIR has five key pillars: renewable energy; every building as a micro-power plant; the use of hydrogen for energy storage and transmission; creating an energy internet to trade green energy; and transitioning transport fleets to electric vehicles.[27] These ideas are starting to be trialled with promising results. The French region of Nord-Pas de Calais has worked with the TIR Consulting Group to create a Third Industrial Revolution Master Plan, an entire road map for steering the region along the lines of these five pillars.

Finally, at my own university, drawing on the pioneering work of Lord Stern in the UK that laid out the economic case for taking action on climate change, a group of researchers have created the Climate Smart Cities framework. They look at the city-wide case, sector by sector, for low-carbon investment options. In Leeds, they found scope for deploying 125 energy efficiency, small-scale renewable and low-carbon measures across the domestic, commercial, industrial and transport sectors. These could add up to a reduction in the city's energy bill by over £1 billion, which could be used to self-finance all this activity. In addition, these would cut its emissions by 36 per cent by 2022, instead of 23 per cent under current predictions.[28]

What is evident from these plans is the availability of sufficient insight, ability and expertise to rapidly and successfully make a just energy transition to a post-carbon city. The task becomes how to galvanise political will, partnerships, public acceptability and economic feasibility to do this. Let's take a look where this is happening.

Zero-Emission Cities

Cities across the world have taken up the post-carbon challenge. Net zero emissions has become a rallying cry. The goal is for urban areas to produce as much energy from renewable sources as they consume. It's a huge task, with end and start points constantly moving. Target setting can be hubris without clearly identified plans, strong leadership and partnership working. There is no single consensus on what needs to be done and groupings of cities are striking out on their own. According to global engineering consultants Arup, 228 global cities, representing 436 million people, have already set GHG reduction goals and targets. Many have adopted net zero emissions targets by 2050 and 80 per cent reductions by 2030.[29] The UK is already legally bound by the Climate Change Act to reduce emissions by 80 per cent by 2050. More than 300 UK municipalities have signed the Nottingham Declaration, which pledges them to systematically address the causes of climate change and to prepare their community for its impacts. The more ambitious task is to get to net zero emissions in the second half of the century, especially given that the UN Environment Programme's 2014 annual emissions gap report states that net zero emissions must happen by 2070 to avoid dangerous warming and to make up for carbon overshoot in the preceding decades.[30] Cities such as Oslo, Antwerp, Melbourne and Copenhagen have risen to this bigger ambition and are pushing for 100 per cent GHG reductions by at least 2050. Moreover, according to C40's Deadline 2020 research, cities should reduce emissions to almost 3 tonnes of CO_2 equivalent per person by 2030 in order to follow the path towards the 1.5°C goal of the Paris Agreement. This will require an overall investment of $1 trillion up to 2050.[31] That's a huge challenge.

Networks of cities such as the C40 Cities Climate Leadership Group, Local Governments for Sustainability (ICLEI) and the United Cities and Local Governments (UCLG) have emerged to share good practice and push city innovation. These networks have come together under the United Nation's Cities and Climate Change programme to form the Compact of Mayors with the aim of creating a common platform to measure city emissions and report to the public. In 2016, the EU Covenant of Mayors came together with the Compact to create a Global Covenant, which now includes over 7,000 cities and 600 million people.[32] This shows the extent to which the energy behind creating a post-carbon society is now rooted at the city rather than national scale.

Clearly, there have been many stalled and misguided attempts along the zero-carbon road such as the much lauded zero-carbon Masdar City in the United Arab Emirates, the as yet unfulfilled promise of new eco-cities across China, as well as promised whole new eco-towns in the UK. But many cities are showing what is possible through coordinated planning. For example, Mexico City has launched an ambitious Climate Action Plan and the measures it contains have the potential to reduce emissions by 10 million tonnes of CO_2 by 2020, representing a decrease of almost 30 per cent relative to the baseline. It was also the first city in Latin America to issue a Green Bond for $50 million.[33] Meanwhile, in 2016, Sydney launched its ambitious Environmental Action Plan, which aims to cut emissions by 70 per cent by 2030 and be a net zero emission city by 2050.

Equally, Vancouver – as the first city in North America to develop a Renewable City Strategy to 2050 – is committing to get 100 per cent of its energy from renewable sources. To achieve this, the city is prioritising reducing emissions from its polluting sectors, buildings and transportation, and increasing the use and supply of renewables. In transport, this includes renewably powered car-sharing fleets and standards to support renewably powered private vehicles.[34] Interestingly, further scrutiny from Simon Fraser University suggested that this kind of decarbonisation plan may be unworkable without drastic measures including phasing out parking spaces for diesel and petrol vehicles from 2025. The World Business Council on Sustainable Development has also launched the Zero Emissions Cities (ZEC) project and initiated three pilot cities in 2015: Amsterdam (Zuidoost) in the Netherlands, Birmingham (Smithfield market) in the UK and San Diego in the USA.[35]

Cities are also taking radical action as they face the risks and impacts of inaction. In the aftermath of Superstorm Sandy in New York in 2012 that left millions without power, there was a growing recognition that its energy infrastructure needs rapid transitioning to help mitigate GHG emissions and build an energy system more resilient to extreme weather events. The Governor of New York State, Andrew Cuomo, sought to rebuild, strengthen and modernise New York's energy system, while bringing economic growth to New York through a strategy called 'Reforming the Energy Vision' (REV). This strategy brought together city authorities to make a clean, resilient and more affordable energy system a reality.[36]

Beyond high-level city planning, much of this kind of thinking is rolling out at a very localised level where impacts can be gauged clearly. And given the growing sophistication and cost effectiveness of micro renewable technologies, the idea of every building acting as its own micro-power station comes ever closer. Early pioneering examples include the Vauban district in Freiberg and Bo1 in Malmo's waterfront in Sweden. The largest net-zero community in the USA is West Village, a mixed-use campus neighbourhood at UC Davis, designed to house 3,500 students, staff and families. Despite technological setbacks and high demand from residents in terms of electrical equipment, it is close to meeting its net-zero design target. BedZed (Beddington Zero Energy Development) has been the UK's pioneering attempt at creating a zero-carbon neighbourhood. It was the creation of architect Bill Dunster. Completed in 2002 at a cost of £15 million, it includes 82 houses, 17 apartments and 1,405 square metres of workspace.[37] The buildings use a passivhaus approach. Originally powered by its own wood-fuelled power station, problems with this led the community to switch to conventional condensing boilers and grid-provided electricity. It also switched from an on-site water treatment plant, which used reed beds to filter waste water, to a membrane bio-reactor filtration system and connection to the municipal sewer system. Locally sourced construction materials, water-saving appliances, green roofs, solar panels and an on-site car-share scheme contribute to further carbon savings. Residents report a strong sense of community, comfortable homes and energy bills up to 80 per cent lower than conventional housing. The project partners, Bioregional, have gone on to develop the One Planet Living neighbourhood concept based on ten principles that taken together can create post-carbon communities of the future. And as I explore more in Chapter 4, in my own project LILAC where I live, we have developed a prototype of low-impact living drawing on a cooperative and cohousing model that reduces a community's ecological footprint through the use of highly insulating and carbon sequestering natural build materials such as lime, timber and straw, as well as developing a sharing economy between neighbours.[38]

The zero-emissions city agenda touches on much more than infrastructure, buildings and transport. It focuses attention on the stubborn and wicked problems of our age, especially around changing the very fabric of our daily lives. What most cities are realising is that beyond the low-hanging fruit of shifts in energy mixes and mobility options, uncomfortable work is required including changes in workplace and consumer behaviour and land zoning modifications. We will simply have to learn to design and live in cities in a different way. We also need to rebalance the energy feast and famine – addressing where the urban energy system is bloated and overused and where it is incredibly unequal and hindering human flourishing. Demand reduction, curtailment and redistribution will remain political hot potatoes, but they are the invisible elements of any meaningful energy transition to post-carbon urban life.

The Civic Energy Revolution

A civic energy revolution is underway. Distributed energy networks, local smart grids and micro-generation all point to how cities can unlock drastically reduced carbon pathways beyond the geopolitical age of big oil, gas and coal.[39] And they can do this in a way that foregrounds social justice and local economic resilience, helping to recycle, redistribute and reinvest the money spent on energy. Cities are particularly challenged by the need for rapid institutional innovation. Today's largely centralised energy generating and supply firms need to be replaced with a connected network of civic players and a greatly expanded role for civil society in delivering distributed low-carbon generation. Local and national states need to play an enabling role in promoting this civic energy revolution. Innovations are flourishing especially in Combined Heat and Power (CHP), onshore wind, solar photovoltaics, anaerobic digestion, energy from waste, smart grids, energy storage technologies, as well as developing the new skills that will underpin these. The new civic energy sector could really mean the age of the large power plant is replaced with a constellation of distributed but highly connected small and medium energy providers. Every home, garden and street becomes a potential place for micro-energy production.

One aspect of this institutional innovation is the creation of municipal energy companies. These locally owned entities can provide cheaper energy, especially in highly uncompetitive consumer energy markets. In the UK, for example, Robin Hood Energy, Bristol Energy and Our Power in Scotland have been established by consortia of local authorities to supply citizens. In public hands, these local energy companies can not only start to sell at a discount, but can also push energy efficiency measures, infrastructure upgrades and investment in local and community renewable generation. This remunicipalisation of energy can have dramatic results. Three cities in the USA run on 100 per cent renewable energy: Aspen, Burlington and Greensburg.[40] At the heart of this achievement are decades of long planning and pro-active publicly owned utilities such as Vermont's Burlington Electric Department (BED).

Germany leads the way in citizen-controlled renewable energy, where around half of the market is publicly owned. The Stadtwerke (publicly owned utility companies) are the keystone and have a rich and long tradition in Germany dating back to the nineteenth century. They now employ nearly 250,000 people and their market share in German energy retail amounts to 46 per cent in electricity, 59 per cent in gas and 65 per cent in heat distribution.[41] Many have operated for decades and drive local innovation, shifting local electricity generation towards a range of renewables – including photovoltaic, onshore wind, hydro, biogas and CHP plants.

For example, through Stadtwerke München, Munich has set the goal of achieving 100 per cent renewable energy supply by 2040, which would make it the first city in the world with over 1 million inhabitants to achieve this. It operates 24 solar photovoltaic power plants and 13 hydro-electric plants, as well as a wind farm, geothermal plants and energy efficient combined heat and power plants. Its district heating network makes heating more efficient. The company has also invested in wind energy around Europe and feeds energy into an integrated European grid to avoid energy waste. Current renewable energy provision saves 1.9 million tonnes of CO_2 and 1.1 tonnes of radioactive waste per year. It continues to invest in renewables to achieve 100 per cent renewable energy provision for the entire city.[42] And there is concerted effort to broaden these efforts. Green City Energy Group, also established in Munich, as well as helping the city to transition to a renewable energy supply, has set up 90 power plants with around 145MW total capacity in Germany, France and Italy.[43]

Below the municipal level, the community energy sector is booming and civil society is leading the way. There are thousands of small- and medium-scale energy cooperatives around the world. According to the World Future Council, in 2015, there were over 2,800 energy cooperatives operating across Europe, and in Australia, there are 45 with 70 in planning. Even in tiny Costa Rica, there are four energy cooperatives with 180,000 members.[44] The Institute for Public Policy Research found that more than 5,000 community energy groups have sprung up around the UK since 2008, providing over 60MW of generating capacity by 2013.[45] Amazingly, these control 15 per cent of the country's energy market. Moreover, the remoteness and ruggedness of Nepal creates the perfect conditions for distributed renewable energy technologies. Fifteen per cent of Nepalese homes are powered from community micro-hydro mini grids and home solar systems.

Powerhouse Incubator, for example, is an umbrella organisation in Oakland, California, which is home to new energy entrepreneurs and start-ups in its co-working space. By providing a collaborative environment where innovation and expertise are shared, and partnerships are forged, Powerhouse is home to nearly 400 people that have to date installed 242MW of solar energy in the USA and abroad.[46] In the UK's capital, Repowering London is a non-profit organisation specialising in facilitating the co-production of community-owned renewable energy projects across south London. The group works with installers and local community groups to develop renewable energy projects and encourages local people to invest in community solar, with profits used for local projects and an annual return for investors. These investments rely on the UK Government's Feed-in Tariff, which pays renewable energy projects for the energy they generate for 20 years. Repowering London collaborates with existing local infrastructure organisations, such as local councils, schools and transportation authorities and has so far created three successful energy cooperatives in Brixton, installing solar energy panels on three apartment blocks in housing estates. In 2015, it also completed Hackney's first community-owned solar energy project, which was the UK's largest community energy project on social housing. In addition, it is working with London-wide organisations to develop Energy Garden, the world's first city-wide community energy, gardening and food growing project.[47]

Scotland's capital is home to a dedicated group of individuals working with Edinburgh City Council to put solar panels on the roofs of public buildings. Edinburgh Community Solar Co-Operative (ECSC) was set up in 2013 and their share offer was launched in September 2015, which raised a staggering £1.4m and offered a 5 per cent return on investments. These kinds of returns exceed the low interest rates offered by bank savings accounts. They are now investigating 25 public buildings to install 1.5 megawatts of solar photovoltaic panels. As well as funding solar panels, the cooperative has a fund for anyone who wants to pursue carbon reduction initiatives, raise awareness or address fuel poverty. Brixton, Bristol and Chester have also seen the emergence of community-owned energy companies.

In the global South, where communities have historically had less access to plentiful energy, this civic energy revolution is taking a different inflection. For example, Kopa, means 'to borrow' in Swahili and provides definition for a solar enterprise based in Nairobi, Kenya. M-Kopa combines micro-credit, solar energy and mobile technology to provide over 500,000 homes across Kenya, Tanzania and Uganda with affordable, sustainable electricity. The company estimates that around 80 per cent of their customers live on $2 a day. Some run small businesses, but the majority rely on small-scale farming. Given the high costs of traditional fuels such as kerosene, M-Kopa offers an alternative in the form of a $200 power system, consisting of solar panels, LED bulbs, flashlight, radio and phone chargers. Clients pay a fractional upfront payment, then a small daily payment for a year after which the system is theirs.[48]

In Banglore, hundreds of thousands of people living in informal settlements still use kerosene as their source of fuel, to the detriment of their physical health and financial security. Pollinate Energy is a social business that trains up micro-entrepreneurs, who they call Pollinators, to install domestic solar lighting systems. This gives communities access to cheaper, renewable energy, providing alternatives to expensive and toxic kerosene. To date, they have supplied over 10,000 people with solar lighting systems, saved over 40,000 litres of kerosene and prevented the emission of 100,000kg of carbon. They are looking to expand operations across 50 Indian cities. These examples are shifting the way we think about and produce renewable energy. With such an array of groups and individuals working in this dynamic sector, all with their own particular objectives but with a shared vision, it is crucial that initiatives can be brought together towards the ultimate aim of creating post-carbon cities. What makes community energy different is that it creates a local energy market that addresses fuel poverty, creates greater ownership of projects, focuses on carbon reductions and aims to retain and generate economic value.[49]

People's Energy Action

Given the strength of the corporate energy sector, unlocking the civic energy revolution will also require resistance from civil society. Those who profit from the fossil fuel age won't simply stand aside. And given that it is such an ingrained and taken-for-granted part of our lives, it will require creative and disruptive ways to displace it. Naomi Klein, in her recent book on climate politics and action, documented the growing diverse movement across the world fighting for a radically different post-carbon, socially just future.[50] We are seeing this in leaps and bounds.

From the anti-fracking campaigners in Scotland and Canada to the anti-coal movements in South Africa and India, civil society is outlining a vision for a post-carbon future that is also socially just. During the 2009 UN Climate meeting in Copenhagen, A People's Declaration was formulated during the People's Climate Summit calling for 'System Change, not Climate Change'.[51] The People's Climate Summit met again during the 2017 UN Climate Change meeting in Bonn demanding the inclusion of civil society and social movements, not fossil corporations, at UN negotiations. For a number of years, the Camp for Climate Action was held in locations in the UK to focus public attention on key carbon battlegrounds. These included a camp at Heathrow in 2007 to highlight the contribution of the aviation industry to climate breakdown as well as urban displacement and air pollution. The 2009 Camp in the City took place outside the European Climate Exchange during the G20 Summit in London to highlight the role of carbon trading as a false solution to climate breakdown. In 2016, in Philadelphia, the Summit for a Clean Energy Revolution saw hundreds of people gather who were working to ban fracking, keep fossil fuels in the ground, stop dirty energy infrastructure and justly transition to 100 per cent renewable energy. The summit was preceded by the Protect Our Public Lands Tour, which brought together different groups directly affected by injustice. Stories of displacement and health impacts were shared, building solidarity and informing a just transition to a post-carbon world. Moreover, a powerful coalition emerged in Hamburg under the banner of Unser Hamburg, Unser Netz (Our Hamburg, Our Networks), which campaigned for, and won, a referendum to remunicipalise the city's energy supply after private sector contracts expired.

Fracking is emerging as one of the unlikely urban battlegrounds. Fracking, or hydraulic fracturing, is the practice of using water in vast quantities mixed with sand and chemical compounds to break underground shale. Often thought of as a largely rural issue, the reality is that many urban areas are sitting on unconventional fossil fuel reserves ripe for fracking. The largest urban oil field in the USA is in Los Angeles county, where more than 1 million people live within five miles of oil wells, which are now being fracked to maintain production levels. Fort Worth in Texas is home to the largest onshore natural gas field in the USA, where the Fort Worth Citizens Against Neighborhood Drilling Ordinance is fighting the spread of fracking activities.[52] Amongst the immediate dangers of fracking on urban dwellers are increased levels of ground-level ozone and contamination of watercourses from methane. In the UK, even when renewables generate more electricity than coal or gas, the move towards fracking keeps marching forward. The epicentre is a stretch of Northern England around the counties of Lancashire and Yorkshire where there are significant underground gas deposits. However, it meets resistance wherever it emerges. Reclaim the Power camps have emerged to oppose local hotspots. Preston New Road near the coastal town of Blackpool has become the unlikely poster-girl where energy firm, Cuadrilla wants to construct the UK's first multi-well shale gas fracturing platform. But the anti-fracking movement is slowly pushing back. Several countries including Germany, France and Scotland have already banned it at a national level, and several US states including Maryland, New York and Vermont have followed suit. However, highlighting the titanic nature of the struggle, communities all over the world attempting to ban fracking are facing legal battles and lawsuits. After the citizens of the Texas city of Denton overwhelmingly voted to ban fracking, the state governor signed a bill into law that prohibits cities from banning it. These are the new urban frontlines where the struggle for a post-carbon city will be played out.

* * *

This is the reality of the post-carbon city: messy, conflictual, contradictory, dangerous. As opportunities for a post-carbon urban world are unlocked, others are locked down. In the terrain of energy, we are not just dealing with technical and infrastructure issues, but also those of power and politics. As I explore in the conclusion, will action be connected and fast enough to avoid the now dangerous effects of staying on the path of high emission urbanism. What more can be done to connect and boost the innovators who are leading the charge towards the post-carbon, net zero civic energy revolution?

3

The Bio City

Cities and nature have become strangely separated. One is associated with work, commerce, industry, consumerism and a host of negative ecological effects such as pollution, noise and dirt. The other is associated with tranquility, leisure, escape and beauty. In this chapter, I challenge this separation between the natural and the urban world. It is part of a whole constellation of false and unhelpful binaries that shape and divide our thinking. Seeing natural systems and urban areas as separate is counter-productive to unlocking sustainable cities. It obscures the complex constellations of resources and ecosystems that constitute city life and the deep interconnections and dependencies between urban dwellers and nature. Cities and nature need to reconnect through a new human–nature urban deal.

I use the term Bio City to point to this and the twin tasks of locking down and unlocking. An urgent lock-down of the destructive ecological tendencies of urban life is required. The air, water and land ecosystems that cities depend upon are being intensely degraded, and resources are being depleted and commodified. There are vast dead zones of alienated urban sprawl and dereliction, retail, highways and industry where residents have little connection with the natural systems that underpin human flourishing. At the same time, I explore the great unlocking, which is slowly emerging through a new restorative and regenerative relationship to urban nature. A constellation of pioneering innovators and ideas including rewilding, permaculture, biomimicry, biophilic design, urban agriculture, continuous productive urban landscapes and blue-green infrastructure are driving these.

Clearly, this is contested ground, with no clear agreement. Caught up in the idea of the bio city and the unfolding future relationship between humans and nature are a whole range of competing visions and assumptions, some utopian and dystopian and others just down right naive or unlikely. When it comes to thinking about the future role of nature in cities, the potential damaging effects of disasters from floods, storms and earthquakes loom large. In this context, nature is seen as a desta-bilising threat that needs to be tamed as it has the capacity to wipe out urban populations and landscapes and set in motion mass migrations. In contrast, in many futuristic and science-fiction visions of future cities, nature is often completely absent, removed by some apocalyptic event, or has become a dominant, resurgent and wild force taking over where human civilisations have diminished or perished. The idea of the bio city also evokes visions of new and unknown human–nature relations based on the efforts of corporate, biotech, life sciences along with artificial intelligence robotics. The potential to create cyborgian, hybrid bioforms and modified plant and animal species looms large.[1]

While the likelihood of these kinds of outcomes is the terrain of speculation, what I want to focus on is a version of the bio city that can represent a new urban–nature deal that can, in the here and now, underpin a shift to sustainability and human flourishing in ways that tackle climate breakdown and social inequality. This is underpinned by a broader social transformation in the relationship between the natural and urban realms, and indeed between humans, nature and other species away from resource extraction, private profit, linear notions of progress and privatisation. In their place come equality, stewardship, nature-based regeneration and restorative cyclical and interconnected relations. A more fundamental rethink of the connections between nature and urban space is required, where social and natural aspects, as well as humans and non-humans find a new basis for mutual coexistence and flourishing. Nature is not just as an aesthetic sideline but is a structural determinant of human flourishing and well-being. The task, then, is to radically reimagine and transcend the false boundary between the natural and the urban world. Moreover, the late inspirational Murray Bookchin and his pioneering work on social ecology reminded us that the deep and corrosive separation between humans and the natural world can only be overcome as we also repair the social fabric between humans.[2] By reducing wealth and social inequalities, and the drive for individual profit, humans can also begin to value and reconnect with each other and the natural world. For too long natural systems have been regarded as a replaceable and free resource at the disposal of the human quest for maximising individual gain within infinitely growing economies. Before we explore the unlocking of this new urban–natural deal, we need to take a brief detour into how we arrived at the excesses of the urban-industrial age.

THE CITY OF INDUSTRY, ENCLOSURE AND PROFIT

Ancient and pre-modern cities emerged and flourished in relative balance with their natural environments. While they developed fairly extensive trading links and communication patterns and were still subject to social inequality and hierarchy, the resources they drew on and the environmental impacts they had were relatively small scale and localised across their hinterlands. Many contemporary cities still retain some of these characteristics. But I don't want to romanticise a particular urban past as representing a golden era of harmony with nature. Rather, I want to focus on the significant step change that has unfolded over the last 250 years under conditions of industrial capitalism that has fundamentally changed the urban experience across the globe. This dynamic started in Europe. As the European feudal order began to break down in the wake of the global reach of colonial networks, slave trading and mercantilist capitalism, the entire social and geographical structure of European societies changed dramatically. The vast wealth accumulated by mercantalist endeavours created fertile ground for the Industrial Revolution and more generally the industrial capitalist city across Europe. Power and land was centralised and deployed to support colonial endeavours and mounting wars between emerging nation states. This new economic system was underpinned by enlightenment beliefs and a civilising zeal, where nature became externalised from the human realm, an object to be conquered, exploited and used for profit.[3] This new approach claimed that through rational scientific endeavours, irrational attitudes associated with nature and theology could be controlled, or at least directed to maximise individual freedom, private property and wealth. We are still living in the legacy of this period and the deep cleavage it created between humans and the natural systems and other species they depend upon.

England became the test case and pioneer for a new urban reality. From the 1760s onwards, the open common field system was subject to a legal process called enclosure whereby the landowning classes appropriated land for private profit.[4] This widespread enclosure and concentration of land led to violent dispossession and forced migration of vast swathes of people into cities. The now depopulated countryside opened up huge new opportunities for wealth accumulation for the landowning classes.[5] Huge gains in productivity drawing on scientific advances in machine use and production processes, especially through coal-based steam power, as well as the availability of new financial credit, laid the foundations for an economy based around the factory system and the development of large-scale industrial production, processing goods from expanding empires and selling to a rapidly expanding middle class at home. The growing working-class population was housed in dense, poor quality accommodation and spent the majority of the day in huge factories manufacturing products for export, or working in heavy steel, coal, or shipbuilding industries. Notwithstanding the scientific, political and cultural developments in this period, the downside of this new urban condition was vast squalor, poverty and inequality. Urban populations increased at a hitherto unprecedented rate in the history of humanity, mainly due to the availability of food and advances in health. For example, in England, on the eve of the Industrial Revolution in 1750, only about 15 per cent of the population lived in towns. By 1900, it was over 80 per cent.[6]

The Industrial Revolution laid down a blueprint for the now global capitalist industrial city. Bewildering new contrasts were generated between the exploding towns and the rapidly depopulating countryside; between smog-filled, polluted cities and the bucolic idyll of the now peaceful (and largely empty) countryside. From these early examples of industrial cities across northern England in Manchester, Liverpool, Sheffield, Newcastle and my home city Leeds, the industrial city spread its reach globally into Europe, North America and Asia. Many of these tendencies of the early industrial city have been enhanced as new industrial sectors around automobiles, chemicals and electronics developed. Most of these early industrial cities have now de-industrialised and shifted wholesale to less polluting service and hospitality sectors. The industrial baton has been passed to cities in developing economies in South America and Asia, where vast export processing activities continue to feed the global economy. Cities throughout the global South are now witnessing huge population growth. These are the world's new megacities, a growing list of urban areas with populations in excess of 10 million including Lagos, Kinshasa, São Paulo, Lahore, Mumbai and Dhaka, with others including Beijing, Karachi and Shanghai exceeding 20 million.[7] Vast swathes of rural dwellers continue to be dispossessed through land concentrations, famines and wars and move to informal settlements on the edge of these rapidly growing megacities. Many find precarious employment in industrial factories, but many more face few employment prospects as megacity population growth is not matched by industrial and employment growth.

Planetary Urbanism

This new form of planetary urbanism is on a categorically different scale and impact in the history of our species on the planet.[8] Indeed, the growth of cities is front and centre of what I referred to earlier as the Anthropocene, a new era in which human activity is now the dominant driving force of global natural systems. More accurately, others have called this the capital-ocene, where capitalism has become the driving force.[9] Rapid urban growth is acutely affecting peri-urban environments, those edge hinterlands where cities expand. The scale and rapidity of peri-urban growth is reaching critical levels especially in terms of its effects on water provision, disaster protection, waste treatment, food production and air quality.[10] Unplanned sprawl in megacities such as São Paulo, Jakarta, Bangkok and Lagos is creating unprecedented stresses on natural systems, which populations depend upon. For example, Jakarta's Citarum River that supplies 80 per cent of the city's drinking water is contaminated with heavy metals and leaves skin rashes on those who use it for washing, while Lagos, a low-lying coastal city which has experienced a 20 per cent decline in wetland areas since the 1970s due to rapid urban encroachment, is experiencing frequent flooding.[11]

This planetary industrial urbanism is perhaps the final turning point of the new human–natural urban deal: finite natural resources seen as free and infinite inputs into a process of ceaseless capital accumulation, ecosystems are widely degraded in their role as usable commodities and treated as dumping grounds, and humans are wrenched from the dense interconnections of natural systems and other species they depend upon. Cities continue to expand and carve out a place with scant regard to the wider bioregions they grew out of. Moreover, the complexities and scale of current industrial growth have led to a complex range of urban environmental problems including: biological pathogens spread from insects, waste, sewerage and water systems; chemical pollutants emerging from ambient air and water pollution and hazardous wastes; soil erosion; deforestation; the impacts of acid rain and ozone plumes; biodiversity loss; raised temperatures; and a litany of environmental hazards including the effects of noise, air quality, overcrowding and physical violence. Fairly sophisticated environmental protection regimes have been developed over the decades, but these are highly variable across the globe. In short, cities have become hazardous places to live in, and one's exposure to them and protection from them is a geographical lottery.

What is left as nature? Outside official city boundaries, it is often little more than industrial nature, peopleless and difficult to access enclosed field systems no different to factories, embedded in commodities and supply chains whose ownership patterns have become concentrated and remote. Pockets have become natural parks, attempts to protect and regenerate natural and wildlife systems. But at the same time, this ossifies the distinction between humans and nature and a particular set of social relations where nature has a distinct aesthetic or commodity value depending on our non-work time. Within city limits, there is an uneasy 'second' nature that is increasingly commodified, based on leisure activities and distilled into various ecosystem services feeding the urban growth imperative.[12] Natural features, be they greenspaces, tree populations, clean air or water, are allocated a price. And it is this price tag that now protects nature. Access can be charged, and they can be traded and sold to the highest bidder like any other commodity. The greater threat is that as natural assets are valued as commodities, they are abstracted; their intrinsic use value is overlooked and our instinctive connection to them is lost.

Relations between humans, the cities they live in and the natural systems they depend upon is an ongoing and complex story. We have not reached the point of extinguishing all vestiges of nature from our urban lives. In fact, as the following sections show, there has been a resurgence. But a central question remains: exactly what kind of relationship with nature do we want to recover in cities? The ossified and enclosed industrial nature of big agriculture? Tamed urban parklands and protected, but ultimately safe and sterilised, wild nature? Nature packaged up as tradable ecosystem services? Beyond these, there is a yet to be defined and emergent new urban–natural deal for human flourishing. It is based on a set of relations between city dwellers and the natural world they can steward and regenerate as a new basis for prosperity.

THE GREEN URBAN AGENDA

No city is merely a concrete desert, void of natural aspects. No matter how alienating urban life can become, it is host to a range of natural features be they animals, plants, water or greenspaces. But that is not to say that all cities have the same green credentials. They are shaped by a complex interplay of history, form and function. Dense, compact cities are far greener by virtue of having a smaller physical footprint where people travel less and make shorter journeys. In contrast, those which have been allowed to sprawl widely over large areas take up significant land areas and often rely on private motorised transport. But the picture is much more complex. Compact cities can have high proportions of high-consuming middle classes, who rely heavily on air travel and external goods, while sprawling global South cities can have relatively low-impact informal settlements, where residents are involved in highly localised but precarious employment. Equally, cities can find themselves swept up by external dynamics. Areas of old industrial cities have been laid to waste as their economic fabric was decimated by the turbulence and unevenness of industrial capitalism. Wild nature can creep back into these voids. As industry retreated in areas such as the US Rustbelt, Germany's Ruhrgebeit and England's northern industrial heartland, old steel works, derelict industrial sites and coalmines have been recolonised by nature.

Moreover, an important part of the story is both the activities of larger top-down master plans from city municipalities and philanthropists in their desire to use natural assets for the benefit of urban citizens and maintain the city's economic base, and more bottom-up practices of activist and community groups. The green city can also grow in less ordered, messy and temporary ways. It is not just in formal parks and greenspaces where nature thrives. Even the smallest places can become natural habitats. Dereliction or pauses in development in vacant lots, as well as in backyards and roadsides, allow glimpses of how nature can temporarily creep back in wherever it is permitted.

The contemporary green urban agenda is nothing new. It is as old as the industrial city. The excesses of early industrialism gave rise to active conservation and environmental movements. Leading figures such as John Muir as well as Charles Darwin's insights from biology and evolution led to attempts to define and protect the rights of nature in the wake of their continued destruction. The Victorian 'back to nature' movement embedded in thinkers such as John Ruskin and William Morris stressed the need to move away from large industrial cities towards more human-scale settlements.[13] Moreover, Romanticism as an artistic and literary movement in the early nineteenth century reacted against growing urban sprawl and pollution.[14] What this meant for cities was a growing awareness and desire to understand and protect nature backed by a whole raft of environmental protection societies and legislation. In particular, as access to the open countryside and former common areas was reduced, legislation focused on creating open public spaces, parks and gardens within cities. In the industrial city, there have been long-standing purposeful attempts to make room for nature, and embed green aspects into the life of the city through, for example, allotment societies, municipal parks, urban woodlands and greenspaces and domestic gardens. There was a practical and public health dimension to this, especially in the face of dangerous levels of air and water pollution and the need to stop the spread of infectious diseases. But it was also driven by moral and philanthropic concerns to provide leisure options for industrial workers and the growing urban middle classes.

From this early interest in preserving nature and bringing it into the industrial city, a much more coordinated international movement has emerged to respond to urban ecosystem degradation and the biospheric, biodiversity and climatic threats ahead. The 1960s and 1970s brought crisis in the post-war economy and a growing awareness that something was deeply flawed with the model of high growth being pushed by the advanced economies of the global North. Rachel Carson's book *Silent Spring*,[15] the 1972 report by the Club of Rome Limits to Growth[16] and the United Nations (UN) Conference on Human Environment more familiarly known as 'the Stockholm Conference', in the same year, as well as the UN's Environment Programme, which came shortly after, were landmark events. The 1980s that followed became a decade preoccupied with sustainable development. How could all this rapid growth in the global economy be handled in a way that would balance social and ecological needs? The Brundtland Commission's 1987 report Our Common Future[17] paved the way for the UN Conference on Environment and Development in 1992, or as it's known the Rio Earth Summit, and the creation of the UN-Habitat-backed Sustainable Cities Programme.

These were landmark events and watershed moments for the urban world. Balancing economic and social priorities with ecological ones has become a mainstay of urban development ever since. The main focus was to embed environmental concerns in urban planning and management and implement the UN Environment Programme's Agenda 21 mission in the heart of every municipality in the world. While this agenda has now largely retreated, it led to a visible shift in debates in cities and towns across the world as they tried to give meaning to sustainable development locally.

Subsequently, much has been achieved through the UN Habitat agenda, which exists to promote socially and environmentally sustainable human development and the achievement of adequate shelter for all. Current efforts focus on its 2030 Agenda for Sustainable Development and its 17 sustainable development goals (SDGs). SDG 11 has become the big focus for 'making cities and human settlements inclusive, safe, resilient and sustainable'.[18] At the Habitat III conference in Quito in 2016, member states signed up to what was dubbed as 'a new urban agenda' to set global standards for sustainable urban development and rethink the way we build, manage and live in cities. Clearly, one of the challenges is translating these grand global initiatives into meaningful and widespread action on the ground. In SDG 11 alone, there are 225 initiatives covering topics as diverse as smart cities, ecovillages and ocean protection.

Nature and Urban Well-Being

There is now greater awareness of the key role nature plays in the direct well-being of city residents. Much focus is being placed on what is called Nature-based Solutions (NbS).[19] These are defined by the International Union for Conservation of Nature as 'actions to protect, sustainably manage, and restore natural or modified ecosystems, that address societal challenges effectively and adaptively, simultaneously providing human well-being and biodiversity benefits'. The overarching goal of NbS is to support the achievement of societal development goals and safeguard human well-being in ways that reflect cultural and societal values and enhance the resilience of ecosystems, their capacity for renewal and the provision of services. NbS are useful specifically because they are designed to address major challenges, such as food security, climate change, water security, human health, disaster risk and social and economic development.

There are so many interconnected benefits of urban nature and a city's green infrastructure, for example: parks with wide tree canopies and minimal paving can reduce the urban heat island effect and city temperatures by up to 2 degrees Celsius; urban woodlands can be a significant carbon sink; trees can be effective in capturing air pollution; green walls and shorter vegetation can considerably reduce air pollution; urban green spaces can store and filter water thus reducing flood risk and improving river water quality; and interconnected greenspaces, especially those using native species, can provide environments for wildlife to thrive in. There are also a whole host of aesthetic, physiological and health benefits associated with urban greenspaces, especially as places of social interaction and leisure. Mathew White and his team from the European Centre for Environment and Human Health at the University of Exeter outlined in a 2012 study that living in an urban area with green spaces has a long-lasting positive impact on people's mental well-being with those living in greener urban areas displaying fewer signs of depression or anxiety.[20] And there are also economic benefits. It was estimated that in the UK, for example, residential and commercial properties overlooking green spaces are valued around 5 to 7 per cent higher than equivalent properties elsewhere,[21] while a University of Pennsylvania study of low-income neighbourhoods in Philadelphia found that newly planted trees boosted sale prices of nearby houses by 2 per cent.[22] On so many levels, reconnecting to nature is a win–win situation. In 2013, Sue Holden, Chief Executive of the Woodland Trust in the UK, stated that the NHS could save £2.1 billion a year if everyone had access to green spaces.[23]

Climate Safe and Resilient Cities

But it's not just about the well-being benefits of these urban ecosystems. In the context of mounting widespread and complex problems, especially extreme weather and resource instability, there is now much attention on creating more resilient and climate-safe patterns of life simply to ensure cities have a good chance of survival. Many cities remain under-prepared for the dramatic potential impacts of climatic breakdown, and how to deal with extreme heat, droughts, floods and other climate-related hazards such as changes in allergens or disease transmission. What exactly a climate-safe or resilient city is remains a key issue.[24] Philip Sutton and David Spratt, for example, in their book *Climate Code Red* present a wake-up call to assess exactly the kind of future we are being locked into under current trajectories. Sensibly, they point out that the climate is not currently safe given that current commitments emerging from the 2016 Paris Agreement set the world on course for well over 3 degrees of warming.[25] We urgently need to know what action is required to hold increases in global average temperatures below 2 degrees Celsius. Through his latest effort, Project Drawdown, the activist and writer Paul Hawken provides some answers. What is required is not just slowing climate change but reversing it through initiatives that rapidly pull carbon dioxide back out of the atmosphere.[26] Cities and their buildings play central roles in this drawdown strategy, especially through moving away from the private car and rapidly greening and reducing the emissions of buildings.

The urban environmental and sustainable development agenda, then, has become intertwined with international protocols and agreements on how to respond to climate breakdown. Cities play a vital role in the implementation and achievement of commitments within international climate change agreements, especially the 2016 Paris Agreement. Cities are technically non-party stakeholders to this agreement, that is to say, they are not the focus of the legally binding commitments. Nevertheless, over 400 mayors were present at Paris, and it is clear that for the successful implementation of the Paris Agreement sub-national and local authorities need to be centrally involved. This is playing out clearly. As the USA pulls out of the UN Paris Agreement, a loose coalition of city mayors, governors, universities and businesses is negotiating to uphold the agreement. What we are seeing is a proliferation of urban initiatives to bolster this movement including the UN-Habitat's City Resilience Profiling Programme, the Rockefeller Foundation's 100 Resilience Cities, C40 Cities Climate Leadership Group and Global Covenant of Mayors for Climate and Energy. As we will see below, the urban environment is being reconfigured through the global attempt to tackle climate breakdown. The potential of climate-safe urbanism is being unlocked in all sorts of novel ways through climate adaptation and innovation districts, where the whole planning of the built environment is focused on the urgent task of adapting to and mitigating the effects of climate breakdown.

Moreover, the issue of urban resilience is deeply challenging. It certainly involves greater resilience of physical infrastructures to withstand turbulence and shocks; but it also requires a fundamental realignment of social and economic systems, so they can be more resilient. And it's not just about withstanding shocks and bouncing back after disasters. Ways of urban living across issues of transport, housing, energy and food need to be developed to build new capacities to reduce those vulnerabilities in the first place. And there is the central issue of resilience for whom? As we make cities more resilient, the benefits need to be broadly shared across, for example, social, religious and racial groups, rather than reinforcing existing urban injustices. The Bio City foregrounds issues of social justice and democratic participation to ensure that all urban areas are as resilient as possible, and political will and resources are equally allocated.

This task of unlocking climate-safe and resilient cities is urgent given the growing number of recent extreme weather events such as Hurricane Katrina, Superstorm Sandy and Hurricane Irma. These are directly exposing the fragility of many cities. What we are learning is that so-called natural disasters are only partly natural. They are products of the poor management of resources, political failure and lock into business-as-usual economics. The burden of these disasters often falls on social groups least able to deal with them. For example, a severe heat wave hit the Indian city of Ahmedabad in 2010 resulting in widespread impacts through dehydration, heat stroke and respiratory problems. Slum residents were especially hard hit and estimates suggest the heat contributed to more than 1,000 deaths in this city of over 5 million people. The high mortality shocked the city and a broad partnership was formed to create India's first Heat Action Plan (HAP) in 2013, which involves community outreach, early warning systems and health care capacity-building. The State Director of Public Health has stated that this HAP reduced mortality by up to 25 per cent.[27]

Reconnecting with and Mimicking Nature

A more fundamental rethink of urban nature is underway. Two ideas – biophilia and biomimicry – are central to this. First, biophilia literally refers to the innate emotional affiliation of human beings to other living organisms and the strong emotional and psychological benefits that are derived through connections to nature.[28] This idea has been brought into the realm of urban design to replicate the experiences of nature into the design process in ways that reinforce that connection. Examples are multiplying in terms of incorporating nature-based design as a method to create healthier spaces in ways that improve well-being outcomes, reduce stress and improve working conditions. This can range from individual household interior design, schools, workplaces, hospitals and hotels incorporating abundant daylight, natural ventilation, plants and greenery. It can also inform urban design more broadly through biophilic neighbourhoods or indeed biophilic cities. At this scale, significant shifts would be required as planning and the management of space is reoriented around a connection with natural and biological systems that we depend upon. We are already surrounded by techno versions of biophilia. Turn on your computer and you are greeted with nature-inspired screen savers depicting forests, grasslands and wildlife aimed at calming your computer experience.[29]

Leading advocates and architectural practitioners of biophilic design, Terrapin Bright Green, have outlined its essential patterns which include connections to nature especially in terms of the presence of views, air, water and light, the use of natural materials in ways that reflect and enhance natural forms and senses, and create spaces that evoke certain senses including withdrawal, mystery, excitement and also risk.[30] Biophilic urban design is an agenda for creating regenerative or restoration urbanism, which proceeds through learning from, connecting to and working with natural systems and creating cyclical and slower relationships between the social and natural worlds. Just as in natural systems, this approach to urban design proceeds from a multitude of small examples that accrue slowly over time and connect together.

Applied at a city scale, the biophilc city would foreground an organic, evolutionary and grass-roots approach to design through observation, trial and error. Urban development would proceed through iterative cycles, where citizens are organically involved in that development process. As a more intimately natural system, the biophilic city would draw on decentralised and hence resilient characteristics of natural systems, in contrast to the centralising and concentrating tendencies of the capitalist industrial city. This is nothing short of a paradigm shift in terms of the relation between urban dwellers and their environments in ways that connect them to light, air, food, nature and community. Biophilic cities would have abundant access to enjoy, benefit and learn from biodiverse, multi-sensory natural environments.[31]

Much of this resonates with the approach of permaculture design, which is based on three interconnecting ethical principles of earth care, people care and fair share. Drawing on these ethical foundations, Permaculture is a whole-systems design approach that uses a natural system inspired approach to decision-making that creates regenerative solutions to design challenges. Attention needs to be given to the different petals of what Permaculture co-founder, David Holmgren, calls the permaculture flower.[32] Each petal represents a basic human need, encompassing issues of community, spirituality, health, waste, shelter, water, energy, food, livelihood and justice. The Permaculture designer and teacher Toby Hemenway has explored how these principles and nature-based whole system design strategies can be applied at the city scale. The exciting thing about this approach is that it makes us aware of the different scales at which we can work. It treats cities as complex adaptive systems where different levels interact through mutually beneficial relationships, from backyards, households, communities, up to whole neighbourhoods, city-regions and bioregions.[33]

These ideas are building an urban movement. The Biophic Cities Project involves 13 partner cities across the globe attempting to foreground nature within the city. Projects include promoting dark skies, coexisting with animals, creating nature soundscapes and maximising natural light. As the founder of the Biophilic Cities Project, Tim Beatley, states they are nature-ful.[34] Birmingham is the UK's first city to join the project and claim itself a Biophilic city, mainly focusing on its efforts to develop an interconnected network of green and blue spaces.

But reconnecting with nature is only one side of this radical new natural urbanism. The second idea is biomimicry.[35] This literally refers to emulating or mimicking the complex engineering and design principles found in the natural world. It is gaining traction within innovation circles, referring to a bio-inspired design method where insights into how nature solves problems can be used to achieve better product performance. The real prospects come from combinations that include innovations in performance that also tackle significant social challenges such as climate breakdown or air pollution. Biomimetic design focuses on the innovations that can occur when natural features are used to improve, integrate and solve challenges. It patiently studies nature to understand what design solutions have emerged. After all, nature is a great teacher. But it teaches us not to just aim to maximise outputs or create one-size-fits-all solutions. It seeks the optimal solution for each given environment and moment. It starts from the user's perspective and how they would design environments to maximise their well-being. Examples of biomimetic design abound: the Japanese Bullet train with a nose inspired by the kingfisher's beak that reduces noise and power consumption while increasing speed; Velcro fasteners inspired by hooks on seed burrs; or the swarming patterns of animals, especially bees and wasps that are assisting with new models of air traffic control and delivery logistics.

Biomimetic design in an urban context is in its infancy, but it has a huge amount to offer in terms of the design, planning and management for urban neighbourhoods and indeed whole city areas that can begin to mimic natural patterns and processes in form and function. There is a growing movement of researchers and innovators supporting the idea. Under the auspices of the CEEBIOS Network, the European Centre for Biomimicry Innovation recently opened in the French town of Senlis.[36] Located in a former military camp, its aim is to support biomimicry research and teaching with the explicit goal of advancing progress towards a post-carbon society. Similarly, Biomimicry UK and its Innovation Lab is spreading the word on how to learn from nature, through workshops, seminars and collaborative research. Greg Keefe, Professor of Architecture at Queens University Belfast, has been at the forefront of research on nature-based urban design, partly through ground-breaking bio-inspired design projects such as BioPort, a utopian vision of a 'Free Energy City' set in Liverpool, where the old dockyards, redundant space, and the Mersey Estuary are transformed into bio-productive algae farms producing bio-fuel which in turn can produce enough electricity to power almost 2 million homes.[37] While these kinds of ideas may never come to fruition, what they represent will at some point be needed, if we are to reconcile the deep and dangerous schism between human and natural systems.

The pioneering green architect, Allison Bernett, stresses that it is easy to mix up biomimicry and biophilia.[38] They sound similar and have similar roots in the environmental movement, but they are concepts with different aims. The exciting aspect for the urban agenda is to explore the applicability of both together – an approach that innovates, solves challenges and improves performance by emulating natural systems, as well as engendering a deep reconnection and love for nature and other species. And it is this last part that is so crucial. Without this deep reconnection, most people will simply not see the rationale for protecting and regenerating nature.

The Biomimetic, Biophilic City

These are not just fanciful ideas – practical examples are emerging. We are beginning to see a proliferation of hybrid natural and built forms through, for example, living walls, rooftop farms, vertical or sky gardens and breathing buildings. These can have significant beneficial effects. For example, urban street canyons refer to the effect created by high buildings lining a street, which can become hotspots for harmful pollutants, such as nitrogen dioxide and particulate matter. A study by Thomas Pugh and colleagues from the Lancaster Environment Centre suggests that strategic placement of vegetation in street canyons can cut air pollution by up to 30 per cent.[39] They can also stop urban overheating and provide effective insulation and shading for buildings, as well as reducing noise pollution. And of course, there are the psychological and aesthetic benefits of being proximate to an abundance of natural greenery.

Green corridors and linear parks can be retrofitted into the existing city. For example, the High Line project in New York transformed an old rail line into a nearly two-mile urban park. It opened in 2014 and became a short cut for walkers and one of the city's favourite parks featuring art installations and places for hanging out.[40] Other cities are following suit including Chicago's 606 Park and Toronto's Bentway, which has slotted 55 outdoor rooms under its Gardiner Expressway featuring farmers' markets, performance spaces and a children's garden. Miami is also building the Underline, a nine-mile linear park underneath its metrorail line. In my own city of Leeds, a community group is attempting to do the same thing on one of Leeds' abandoned Victorian train viaducts. The Madrid Rio project was one of the most exciting urban reclamation projects in Europe – burying a former ring road to create over 600 hectares of parkland. Efforts are being made not just to create greenspaces, but to create interconnected green corridors. For example, the All London Green Grid (ALGG) is the green infrastructure strategy for London, which sets out a vision to create an interconnected network of green and blue spaces across the entire city.[41] It is this interconnection that is so important in terms of creating space for biodiversity to move more extensively.

Singapore is one of the pioneers of placing nature at the heart of its planning and urban design process. As a self-labelled garden city, it now prefers to call itself 'the city in a garden'. To realize this vision of living in an urban park, Singapore implemented a landscape replacement policy whereby any greenery removed during construction has to be reinstated as part of the development. It is estimated that the amount of urban greenery has been at least doubled, but mainly through sky gardens. The city has also built nearly 300km of park connectors to create deeper connections between parks and neighbourhoods.[42]

It is not just streets that are turning green but whole buildings. Reputedly the world's largest vertical garden is in Bogota, Colombia, on a building called the Santalaia, a nine-storey residential building featuring 85,000 plants and using recycled water to irrigate them through 42 water stations. Santalaia is a giant air purifier and carbon sink absorbing the annual carbon dioxide emissions from over 700 cars.[43] In Milan, il Bosco Verticale is one of the most comprehensive vertical green walls in the world. It is a living example of city design that engenders a reconnection to nature whilst solving challenges and improving performance by emulating natural systems. Opened in 2014, it comprises two towers that is home to 1,000 different species of plants, made up of 480 large and medium trees, 300 small trees, 11,000 perennial and covering plants and 5,000 shrubs. An estimated 1,600 species of birds and butterflies interact with the Vertical Forest.[44] The vegetation was specially selected according to the optimum conditions required for each plant and was the result of three years of botanic study. This coverage helps mitigate smog and air pollutants, produce oxygen, moderate building temperatures, slow excessive winds, and attenuate noise, and given the two towers contain over 100 apartments, they reduce urban sprawl. The wonderful aspect about these innovations is that they are simple and based on ancient principles of vertical growing which have been evident in human culture for centuries, epitomised, for example, by the fabled Hanging Gardens of Babylon.

Work is also underway on vertical forests in eastern China on two towers that will be covered in 1,100 trees and 2,500 cascading plants and shrubs. The project in Nanjing City will include offices, school, shops and an exhibition space. It is hoped that the towers, designed by Italian architect Stefano Boeri, who is also responsible for Milan's il Bosco Verticale, will absorb 25 tonnes of CO_2 every year and produce 60 kilogrammes of oxygen each day. Those behind this project hope to build thousands more around the world to help offset deadly urban air pollution, especially in China.[45]

Internationally recognised standards are now emerging to promote this green building movement. The International Living Building Institute's Living Building Challenge is a green building certification programme and sustainable design framework for bio-inspired buildings. It uses the metaphor of a flower because, as the Institute states, the ideal built environment should function as cleanly and efficiently as a flower. The Living Building Challenge requires a project to meet 20 specific imperatives within seven performance areas including site and sustainable mobility options, water use and recycling, renewable energy, health, materials, equity especially in terms of quality and size of workspaces, and beauty. The Institute has also established the Biophilic Design Initiative to promote the practice of connecting people and nature within our built environments and communities.[46]

The Bullitt Center in Seattle, built by the Bullitt Foundation, is an attempt to demonstrate what a building might be, if it was designed alongside biomimetic principles. Officially opened on Earth Day in 2013, it is claimed to be the greenest commercial building in the world. It came with a $300m price tag but also a 250-year lifespan and achieved the goals of the Living Building Challenge. It is designed to be energy and carbon neutral, with a water and sewage processing system independent of municipal systems. It is the first commercial building in the USA to earn FSC Project Certification and amazingly enough has no parking spaces, only bike racks. The aims of the Bullitt Center are broader than the footprint of the building. It is located in what is called the Capitol Hill Ecodistrict, part of a broader vision to create neighbourhood-level sustainability.[47]

The exciting thing is that these new connections with nature can unlock seemingly intractable problems. For example, Martin Pauli, an architect and materials specialist at Arup made the revealing discovery that the asparagus plant is extremely effective at absorbing pollutants.[48] This has led to insights that green façades often along the edge of roads and walkways are extremely under-utilised systems but could be a key element in improving urban air quality. High pollution absorbing plants could feature in borders next to schools, for example, where air pollution linked to cars is having immediate negative effects on children's health.

Moreover, researchers at Nottingham Trent University are studying the structure of termite mounds that could reveal new sustainable construction methods.[49] Studies of mounds built by termites in India and Namibia found that they enable stale and fresh air to be exchanged while maintaining a comfortable temperature. Researchers are exploring if it is possible to mimic these structures to create buildings with walls that breathe in the same way and reduce the need for central heating or air conditioning. Similar research is being undertaken on algae, a natural resource that can potentially be used to create new sources of food and fuel. Photosynthesis allows the algae to store light energy in a form of chemical energy that can be converted to electricity. Research is being directed towards the potential of algae-powered light bulbs and even whole buildings. The exciting challenge is whether this could power whole urban neighbourhoods. The world's first algae-powered building called BIQ has been built in Hamburg. It has an algae façade made of bio-reactive louvers that enclose the algae. These louvers allow the algae to survive and grow faster than they would otherwise, while also providing shade for the interior of the building. Additionally, the bio-reactors trap the heat energy created by the algae, which can then be harvested and used to power the building.[50]

The Blue-Green City

One of the key challenges of the bio city is finding new ways to live around water and especially water-related crises. In terms of creating cities that are more drought and flood resilient in the future, the real challenge is to blend, and ultimately replace, conventional approaches to water management around centralised piped and energy-intensive grey infrastructures with more novel blue-green infrastructures. Out goes the 'pave, pipe and pump' approach of burying expensive infrastructure below ground; in comes novel socio-technical solutions visible above ground where residents learn to interact with them.

This is the blue-green city agenda. As Colin Thorne, director of the Blue-Green cities research programme at Nottingham University in the UK states, it aims to recreate a naturally oriented water cycle, while contributing to the amenity of the city by bringing water management and green infrastructure together.[51] This is achieved by combining and protecting the hydrological and ecological values of the urban landscape, while providing resilient and adaptive measures to deal with flood events. In practice, blue technologies based around small footprint high-efficiency devices such as storm water filtration, attenuation and rainwater capture systems are combined with distributed and locally relevant green infrastructures. These come in many forms: urban rain gardens, green roofs, porous pavements, bio-filtration ponds, urban wetlands, swales and sustainable drainage systems. The blue-green city foregrounds what is called water-sensitive or water-centric urbanism. This is part of the shift away from old paradigm thinking associated with the centralised industrial city. It reminds us that the city is an inter-connected system, with its own metabolism of complex flows, inputs and outputs. The design task is to integrate these various systems at the neighbourhood scale and to maximise the ecological and social benefits from them.

Some great examples are emerging. In the early 2000s, the US city of Portland began its 'grey to green initiative', which included the implementation of water-sensitive design through river restoration, and parks and ecosystem rejuvenation. This agenda was driven by the need for greater flood risk management and to engage communities further in the multiple benefits of blue-green urban development. Meanwhile, Philadelphia has embarked on a 25-year plan to install thousands of rain gardens and permeable surfaces to allow rainwater to seep into the ground rather than run off into sewers and streams. Chicago, which is facing 40 per cent more winter precipitation over the coming decades, is responding by building green alleys, pavements that are permeable to storm water so they can drain faster. One of these is the two-mile Pilsen Sustainable Street, billed as the 'greenest street' in the USA, featuring bioswales that filter and absorb polluted run-off rainwater. Meanwhile, the Chicago architects UrbanLab are designing for the Chinese government what are being called Sponge Cities in the low-lying Hunan province. Major buildings are placed on islands in a lake connected by eco-boulevards. Many flood prone areas such as Dhaka in Bangladesh are using amphibious architecture, to place floating buildings in densely populated areas that can house essential amenities such as classrooms and toilets.

In Denmark, Copenhagen's Saint Kjelds quarter is billed as the world's first climate adapted neighbourhood, which is foregrounding water-sensitive design. In the face of heavier rainstorms and repeated 100-year floods too big for the city's sewers, the city embarked upon an ambitious redesign of the neighbourhood, which involved reducing 20 per cent of street surface and introducing dual purpose design including bicycle paths that act as storm water channels, and water towers, green roofs and canals that carry water out of the neighbourhood to the harbour. Innovative features such as cloudburst boulevards and retention zones mean that flood water stays in the neighbourhood longer before it safely drains away. Clearly, behaviour change is key to these adaptations as residents have to learn to live around water for periods of time. Community engagement is key allowing residents to adapt and plant the green spaces. The task remains a challenging one, not just in terms of infrastructure but also in terms of cultural shifts.

A technique called 'daylighting' urban waterways is a novel part of water-centric urbanism. There is an emerging movement that is attempting to recover and reintegrate lost rivers that run beneath our cities. As well as giving people the opportunity to interact with the blue city, the process of de-culverting reveals a new urban ecology and re-establishes previously buried natural patterns. In the city of Sheffield in the UK, for example, a section of the river Porter has recently been daylighted with a pocket park added. By reintegrating rivers into the urban landscape, there is the potential for a new relationship between people and nature to emerge. This is an important part of the great unlocking, the process of reactivating post-industrial zones in cities, where residents and workers might have little connection to the natural systems that underpin their ability to flourish as humans.

Urban Farming

Growing food has long been a part of city life but the multiple challenges facing cities is encouraging a renaissance. Urban agriculture offers multiple benefits in terms of ecological footprints, food miles, better quality food, greater connection between consumers and producers, spin-off opportunities for employment and income, the reuse of underused land, as well as health and well-being effects for participants. It also foregrounds the crucial issue of food justice and food sovereignty to allow urban dwellers to take back control over where their food is produced. Given the complexities of finding room to produce food in cities, urban food growing comes in so many forms including rooftop and vertical farms, community supported agriculture schemes, allotments and community gardens. All of these encourage the creation of more compact urban forms, which are highly connected to rural hinterlands. Linking these is the idea of Continuous Productive Urban Landscapes (CPUL). Outlined by the architect André Viljoen, CPULs are a way of integrating food growing into the design of cities through creating green fingers that join together existing sites into linear landscapes that connects the urban out to the rural.[52]

For example, ØsterGRO farm is located in Copenhagen's densely populated Østerbro neighbourhood where its founders had the vision for an organic rooftop farm. In collaboration with a rural partner farm, ØsterGRO grows and distributes food for its 40-member community-supported agriculture (CSA) scheme. The 600m^2 farm produces vegetables, eggs and honey and has an on-site restaurant, market and workshop. In my own city Leeds, the social enterprise Growing Better is dedicated to addressing mental health through growing food. Their urban farm provides a supportive working environment for people facing a range of mental health challenges and contributes to the sustainable, local and independent food ecosystem, reducing food miles, supporting micro-farming and encouraging healthy eating. They also have a micro-scale vertical farm, which utilises derelict land to grow high-value salad crops.

Urban farming is also being used as a way to reverse urban decline. The long, slow decline of the US city of Detroit was the result of a fragile housing market and a turbulent manufacturing sector, with this fabled global Motor City suffering huge losses over recent decades. With over 1 million taxpayers leaving Detroit since major car manufacturers closed, the city took the easiest – but most short-sighted – option of bulldozing crumbling neighbourhoods. Since 1960, over 200,000 housing units have been razed to the ground. Yet many residents stayed, determined to rejuvenate the places they called home. This vacant land represented fertile ground to initiate an agricultural revolution in the city. Urban farming projects have emerged in this context. More than just a food resource, many of the initiatives taking place aim to engage community members in the practice of growing, to give people skills and empower them to intervene in broader issues of food insecurity and build a grassroots network of agricultural projects. One such project is the Michigan Urban Farming Initiative (MUFI), which was set up in 2011 and has grown over 22,000 kilogrammes of produce since then to use urban agriculture as a platform to promote education, sustainability and community empowerment.[53] They also see this as a broader model for redeveloping other urban communities facing disinvestment. The creation of these productive landscapes is an exciting shift in the attitude towards a written-off city. Detroiters are proving the critics wrong and becoming stewards of their urban landscape – moving away from abandonment towards an interconnected relationship with nature.

The R-Urban project in Paris is an example of an integrated experiment in deploying an urban commons approach to enhance neighbourhood resilience. It is made up of four functioning sections based on the philosophy of 'produce what we consume and consume what we produce'. First, there is AgroCité, a unit of urban agriculture, which consists of a micro-experimental farm, community gardens, educational and cultural spaces and devices for energy production, composting and rainwater recycling. Second, RecyLab houses recycling equipment for urban waste turning them into materials for eco-construction. Third, Ecohab is a residential cooperative unit consisting of a number of experimental units and community spaces which are self-built. Finally, AnimaLab is a domestic farm. The project was first established in Colombes in north-west Paris and has recently relocated to Gennevilliers.[54]

Community supported agriculture (CSA) is part of this growing social movement that encourages urban and rural citizens to share responsibility for the land where their food is grown as well as for how it is produced. In simplest terms, CSA is a partnership between agricultural producers and consumers. Members are shareholders and pay a fee at the beginning of the growing season to meet a farm's operating expenses for the upcoming season. Consumers get high-quality food produced with a strong sense of care for the land and environment. Meanwhile, farmers can plan their crops better and feel secure in their livelihoods, knowing that they will receive a fair price and how many people they need to feed. The USA has been the focus for growth for these kinds of solidarity-based food partnerships. There are 7,000 CSAs in the USA with the largest, 'Farm Fresh To You' in Capay Valley California, having 13,000 shareholders.[55] The Quebec CSA network has more than 100 farms and there are at least 100 CSAs in the UK, many in towns and cities.[56] But equally, there are now CSAs across Africa, Asia and Latin America, all of which tap into the desire to develop small-scale organic family farming and increase local food sovereignty as a response to the problems associated with global intensive agriculture. Urgenci is the international network for CSAs, which provides resources and support across the world.

The Wild City

It can feel as if cities are only home to one species – us humans. But a rich array of wildlife has always been part of city life.[57] For a whole range of animals, urban areas are simply another habitat to occupy. Beyond the more familiar sight of pigeons, foxes and squirrels, cities are home to a multitude of animal species including migratory birds, woodland creatures and insects. But the question becomes to what extent can non-human animal species coexist with humans, given the overwhelming speed and scale of contemporary urban development. As urban growth continues apace, the human world encroaches on the habitats of animals. There are many aspects to this and it pulls in different directions. Animal populations such as crows, doves, foxes and even leopards in some Indian cities are thriving from urban expansion and the new food sources on offer. But the big threat is habitat loss. This takes the form of tiny everyday acts like the loss of urban residential gardens, densification through infill development and increasing levels of air and water pollution. It also takes the form of the relentless expansion of urban areas into new territory. Across the global South, this peri-urban expansion is leading to rapid levels of habitat loss. Species that simply cannot move as fast as urban expansion will disappear. Larger animals including wolves, deer, bear and wild boar are now more frequent visitors to cities, usually on the hunt for food as their non-urban habitats are squeezed.

There is a broader practical and philosophical dilemma that concerns the ongoing and future relationship between different species on our planet – how we understand and respond to our interdependent lives. At its maximum extent, it is estimated that 100 million different species coexisted on our planet. But due to the impact of just one of these – humans – up to 100,000 species are becoming extinct annually. Some researchers point to a potential biological annihilation in the near future given that the number of animals that once coexisted with humans has fallen by up to 50 per cent.[58]

Rebalancing this relationship is part of the bio city agenda. This is not only in terms of addressing habitat loss and incursions. But it is also about re-embedding the interconnected relationship between species within the city. This is not simply an abstract task. It is one that a growing urban rewilding movement is addressing head on.[59] Removing human-made barriers to nature, restoring the original form and function of natural landscapes, and replacing lost elements is offering multiple and tangible benefits to humans and animals. Introducing certain animals can help facilitate the growth and maintenance of a diverse range of plant species. They provide an important and free ecosystem service. Wild natural areas are also places where animals can forage and exist in expansive areas. Many health studies also show that proximity to nature and animals improves our mood, reduces stress and increases immunity. There is also an important animal perspective on green corridors. They open up opportunities not just for the transfer of people or nutrients, but also animals across previously disconnected and dangerous grey urban spaces.

None of this is an easy task. On a practical level, it will be very difficult for humans to coexist peacefully with a greater number of animals, especially larger more threatening ones. Their novelty will be misinterpreted as invasion but it begs the broader philosophical question about rights and ownership. Who and what exactly is the city for? A co-presence and abundance of other animal species reminds urban dwellers that we are neither the only, nor the superior, species on the planet. We are, and have always been, part of and co-dependant on the natural world. This recognition, as well as greater social and technological innovation, will be required in order to establish a prosperous and sustainable urban future. Very simply, if we don't spend time in and with nature, why would we be motivated to protect it?

* * *

This is the bio city agenda. What I have represented is a partial and ongoing account. There is much more to be said on every aspect I have introduced. But the scale of the task is clear. Reversing the trend of industrial urbanism confronts us with a complex and seemingly inevitable social and political history that incorporates colonialism, imperialism, capitalism and technology. Beginning to undo this requires recovering a very different human–natural deal and rethinking the very philosophical rationale for the city, its economies, infrastructures and institutions, flows and connections that define it. But innovators across the world from all sectors are beginning to unlock the potential of nature in the city. The question remains whether action can be fast enough to respond to the urgent threats of climate breakdown, water stresses, pollution and biodiversity loss.

4

The Common City

If anything gives meaning to cities, it is the rich encounters and dense networks of relationships they offer. It is here that we enact our democratic lives, undertake economic transactions that allow us to flourish and build nourishing social relations with others. It is where we all come together. Cities are the ultimate experiment in creating the common, places of collective encounter in which people negotiate access to resources and relationships that they depend on. Over the centuries, cities have developed institutions, policies and spaces, which attempt to create the conditions for this flourishing in common.

But in this current phase in human history something is deeply amiss. The contemporary urban experience is far from common. Paradoxically, in spite of the global spread of the urban condition, in many ways it is becoming deeply uncommon. The signature characteristic is the significant and growing gap between the haves and the have-nots, a deep and lasting sense that for vast swathes of the urban population what is happening is not for them.[1] Institutions for civic democracy have become detached, over-bureaucratic, ossified into silo thinking and actions and public trust in them continues to plummet. Urban economies no longer attempt to distribute wealth and ameliorate income and social polarities. Instead they largely function to facilitate large capital enterprises so they can extract value from local economies, suck out and concentrate wealth within extra local corporate supply chains.

In this chapter, I use the term common city to return to the twin dynamics of lock-down and unlocking. We need to be brave to name and counter the aspects of urban life that continue to constrain and hold back a more progressive basis for human flourishing. The task is vast and interconnected. It requires action across a growing web of alliances that stretches between and through the political, civic, academic and business worlds. It requires a new set of expectations and narratives about how our urban communities, economies and civic institutions function. In this great process of re-commoning, radically new ways of doing democracy need activating, novel approaches established to unlock the potential of land and resources that communities hold, and the power of a more participatory, collaborative and egalitarian urban economy require super-charging.

THE UNCOMMON CITY

It is difficult to talk about one particular democratic experience in cities. They vary so wildly according to history, culture and context. It is no longer the case – if it ever was – that municipal authorities are able to speak for, and govern, the range of diverse and competing interests and localities that make up urban areas. Current trends point towards a much more complicated task for those attempting to govern cities. City politicians across the world face a perfect storm of increasingly complex and interconnected challenges alongside reduced ability to respond to them. Problems persist and combine across issues of, for example, poverty, inequality, population growth, ageing, resource scarcity, environmental degradation, climate change and security threats. City leaders respond from within institutions that seem ossified and out of date, plagued by short-term and siloed decision-making, low citizen engagement, the exclusion of diverse voices, and power imbalances between a largely ascendant free-market oriented private sector and weakened civil society and public sectors. Most acutely, in the continuing era of fiscal austerity, municipalities are engaged with the reality of simply doing less with less, often reduced to the role of commissioning goods and services rather than setting a strategic vision.[2]

These changes are part of a wider and longer story. The structure and function of urban societies and their relationship with state and capital has been subject to significant turbulence over the last 40 years. In Europe and North America, as the welfarist, Keynesian model of growth unravelled in the 1970s, a new orthodoxy based around free market monetarism gained the upper hand, through the emergence and consolidation of what is called neoliberalisation.[3] Out went wage controls, the structural dominance of industrial production, unionised labour, national control over money flows and exchange rates. Advanced economies took a structural turn towards financial and service activities, the freeing up of capital flows and exchange rates, and the private ownership and commodification of assets and resources. New Public Management (NPM) scholars have highlighted that market-based solutions now extend into public sector arenas where these approaches might not previously have been seen as legitimate.[4]

The Neoliberal City

This had dramatic effects on cities. Given neoliberal economics largely shape our world, and our world is increasingly urban, it is no surprise that we are faced with the age of the neoliberal city.[5] While urban economies have remained sources of vitality, prosperity and creativity, how they do this has fundamentally changed. Cities sit squarely at the heart of a big capital, globalised, competitive, pro-growth economic model. They have increasingly become locked into a fast money, highly volatile inward investment economy, dominated by competition between cities, big brands, zero-hour contracts and low pay, poor skills and educational opportunities. Much of this isn't geared towards the challenges ahead such as community resilience, reducing carbon emissions or narrowing income inequalities. Instead, it instrumentally feeds non-local economies and firms, extracting surplus value from places and stripping them of essential resources. As the Marxist geographer David Harvey pointed out back in the 1990s, cities have fundamentally shifted their role from 'urban managerialism' to 'urban entrepreneurialism', where city governance has become as much about managing its brand to attract footloose private capital as its social role in providing basic goods and services.[6]

The contemporary picture of urban inequality makes for grim reading, but it is a complex and variegated one. There are significant gaps between cities. Many knowledge intensive metro areas are experiencing wage and employment growth especially in high tech, digital, health and education sectors. Meanwhile, vast swathes of smaller cities, often in the shadow of more prosperous and larger metro areas, have been unable to find a role in this new economy, especially those struggling with the rapid decline of industry. But there are also persistent gaps within cities as central areas prosper at the expense of poorer outlying neighbourhoods. This is particularly the case in informal settlements, or slums, which are a world apart from surrounding neighbourhoods. According to the UN, nearly 900 million people, or one-third of the urban population of the developing world, live in slums.[7] What is evident is that the still unshakable belief in wealth trickle-down is deeply entrenched. UN-Habitat tracks the most unequal cities in the world using the Gini index, which measures inequality. The higher the level, the more that wealth is concentrated in the hands of fewer people, and it sets an international alert line at 0.4. What urban level data sheds light on is the scale of the urban divide. In its 2010 State of the World's Cities report, cities such as Bogota, Nairobi and Mexico City came out worse, with Johannesburg having the greatest income divide at over 0.7. The USA has the most unequal cities amongst the so-called developed nations with Miami, Atlanta and New York over the alert line and fairing as badly as many developing world cities.[8]

Changes to the urban space are also stark. We are now familiar with how corporate brands such as Nike and Starbucks have extended their reach into high streets and malls across the world. The New Economics Foundation in the UK has tracked this creeping corporate takeover of high streets through its 2007 report Clone Town Britain, documenting how the increasing domination of large chain stores is leaving communities and high streets vulnerable to economic shocks.[9] This corporate saturation of urban space is being logically extended to whole urban quarters, especially through corporate-funded Business Improvement Districts. The incisive urban sociologist, Saskia Sassen, points to the growing concentration of ownership of central urban areas especially in global cities such as New York, Beijing and London, since the 2008 financial crash.[10] Large-scale buying of vast chunks of urban space by global corporate investors is underway leading to a shift from mostly small private to large corporate ownership, and from public to private. Gentrification has become the watchword where cities become geared up to the retail, work and leisure needs of salaried workers and those with access to plentiful credit. Gentrification is the blunt end of the corporate takeover of urban land, assets and resources.[11] But it works so well as it has colonised our thought processes and the very way we think about cities. It is seductive. Central areas, historic cores, waterfronts are transformed into hermetically sealed playgrounds. While they are beautifully marketed and crafted as if for the many, they only function for the few. Never before has the economic, social and cultural divides been so prominent between the urban haves and have-nots.

This turn to urban neoliberalisation is also a broader set of cultural changes that creates the frame of reference of what is possible, creating a taken for granted ordinariness of events happening around us. The political scientist, David Crouch, called the current era one of 'post-democracy', where largely unaccountable, opaque and distant corporate power takes control over the daily lives of citizens, as well as the resource and land base of urban areas.[12] Cities are now highly connected to extra-local networks and identities, especially transnational and private capital flows. The question has to be posed whether cities are any longer run in the interests of their citizens.

We have got to a point where contemporary forms of urban democracy are simply not calibrated to respond to the challenges ahead. Experiences more often relate to political disengagement, hierarchy, tokenism, centralisation as well as oppression and surveillance. Back in 2006, during the influential Power Inquiry in the UK, Baroness Helena Kennedy stated that 'politics and government are increasingly in the hands of privileged elites, as if democracy has run out of steam'.[13] City administrations are rarely governed beyond an established party political elite. City or metro mayors offer some new opportunities for more direct political engagement, but they can also enhance tendencies towards charismatic and personality politics rather than radically decentralising power to neighbourhoods. More worryingly, urban dwellers in large parts of the majority world from Syria to Sudan, Ukraine to Yemen, live in fear of occupation, paramilitaries and war.

These aspects have direct impacts on our wellbeing and quality of life, which is tightly bound to the immediate localities where we live. Wellbeing ranges across a number of factors including security and crime, social networks, transport options, employment opportunities, the availability of local goods and services, especially those relating to health care and education, and access to good quality green spaces, as well as levels of noise and air pollution. Approaches to place-making are severely lacking. They have become subject to abstract and alienated planning systems, scarred by bureaucracy, corporate greed, car dominance and concentrated land ownership. Valuable land that could be used for food, housing or local employment is locked out of use by speculative asset managers hoping to realize higher values. In his study of who owns Britain, Kevin Cahill estimates that 69 per cent of Britain is owned by 0.6 per cent of the population; and while only 158,000 families own 41 million acres of agricultural land, 24 million families live on the 4 million acres of urban land.[14] In a similar vein, a US Department of Agriculture report in 2016 shockingly stated that the five largest landowners, all white, own more rural land than all of black America combined, that's over 40 million people.[15]

Land is increasingly an asset to be traded to the highest bidder rather than a common resource to underpin human flourishing and community resilience. If there is one particularly pernicious aspect that is acutely felt at the neighbourhood level, it is land banking. This is a practice where large-scale speculative developers retain large portfolios of land to restrict and control supply, maintain higher values and offer maximum returns for shareholders. An investigation by *The Guardian* newspaper in the UK on land banking revealed that in 2015 the UK's biggest house-builders including Berkeley, Barratt, Persimmon and Taylor Wimpey are sitting on 600,000 plots of land with planning permission – that equals four times the total number of homes built in 2015 and a pipeline of six years of building work.[16]

So we live in deeply uncommon urban times. As some urbanities continue to enjoy the visible signs of urban renaissance, the corporate takeover of cities silently continues. But people are a city's greatest asset and this is increasingly so in such divided times. The common city is being built all the time, through practices of both creation and resistance.[17] As I explore below, the task is to unlock it, rapidly and at scale.

BUILDING THE COMMON CITY

As is now becoming obvious, the story of cities is dynamic, complex and multidimensional. They are neither stuck on negative trajectories of decline and despair, nor are they utopian idylls. Amongst the seemingly unshakable corporate city, the common city continues to grow and spread. The common is a powerful metaphor and political tool. Much of this concept dates back to the enclosures of English land, and dispossession of peasants from that land, just before the onset of the Industrial Revolution in the early to mid-eighteenth century. Dispossessing the poor, peasant and indigenous peoples of vital resources and direct attacks on their livelihoods, then, have underpinned efforts to defend the common for many centuries. But today the common refers to much more than simple bounded territories. It also encompasses physical attributes of air, water, soil and plants as well as socially reproduced goods such as knowledge, languages, codes and importantly information.[18]

Looking beyond these basic physical attributes, the common is a complex social and political entity underpinned by particular social practices, relationships and forms of governance. The common, then, can also be considered as a social relationship between commoners who build, defend, reproduce and collectively own it. Understanding the common is important given that contemporary patterns of capital accumulation increasingly seek to dispossess the poorest and most marginal groups in society of the vital resources they depend upon and undermine their livelihoods. To open up new areas for profit, capitalism advances by further enclosure, appropriation and dispossession of land, resources and life-worlds. What we are witnessing in the contemporary moment of capitalist development globally is a particularly virulent form of primitive accumulation ushering in new forms of enclosure akin to those seen in Europe during the eighteenth and nineteenth centuries. It is expanding into a whole host of new areas such as previously protected public services in health, education and housing as well as the Internet, plant patents, biospheric resources, and most recently, the carbon cycle.

Reclaiming the Urban Common

Cities are the ultimate common. As the urban condition becomes the hallmark for the majority of humanity across the planet, so too the city becomes thoroughly characterised by both the powerful forces of capital accumulation as well as the practices and potentials of the common. Everything is a potential common; everyone is a potential commoner. It's a question of political organisation. Bringing the idea of the common into play in the city sharpens analysis of the task at hand – the decoupling of work and life in the contemporary city from the logic of capital. Finding new ways to produce urban space and organise socially useful production can begin to form the bedrock of challenging capitalism at the everyday level. It is important to note that this is different to the broader trends towards a sharing economy. Practices of commoning go much further than sharing. Commoning generates and circulates social wealth in ways that have the potential to erode private property relations, individualism and the exchange value of commodities.

The community level represents a particularly productive laboratory for rebuilding the urban common. Examples abound of community and place-making which challenge the uncommon, corporate city and show glimpses of the urban common beyond the status quo. Novel forms of eco and community-led housing, attempts to revive local places, neighbourhoods and high streets, as well as reclaim land all demonstrate a bank of skills and knowledge that is being unleashed to build the common city.

Putting resources and assets back into community hands through community ownership shows how resources can be managed in common. The important aspect is that this is different to, and it sits between, public and private ownership. Community ownership is becoming a bulwark against forced disposals of public assets by strapped municipalities and the profit-seeking activities of private capital. Community organisations are seen to have a special role in their places as anchors. Their aim is common wealth building. They retain and re-spend local money, favour local employment and reskilling, and are more democratically accountable.

From town halls and schools, to public houses and swimming pools, communities are organising to raise funds and bring assets back into community ownership. Pioneering examples such as Coin Street in London show what can be achieved. In the 1980s, a group of local residents formed Coin Street Community Builders to provide affordable accommodation on London's South Bank, which is now one of the highest value areas of central London. More recently in Berlin in 2007, residents from an inner-city area bought an old printworks and converted it into a not-for-profit cultural and business centre called ExRotaprint.[19]

These activities form a diverse global movement. In contrast to the land banking model of the volume corporate builders, Community Development Corporations (CDCs) have risen to this task. They are not-for-profit, community-based organisations which aim to revitalise the areas in which they are located, typically low-income neighbourhoods suffering from negative spirals of decline and disinvestment. In the USA, there are nearly 5,000 CDCs located across every state that produce almost 100,000 homes a year. These community anchor organisations are supported by Community Development Financial Institutions (CDFIs), which provide credit and financial services to people and communities underserved by mainstream lenders. Similarly, there is a focus on supporting community businesses as they are locally rooted, trade for the benefit of the local community, are locally accountable and offer broad impact across a range of sectors and groups. In England, the national charity Power to Change has estimated there are over 7,000 community businesses,[20] while the Locality network of community organisations represents over 600 community members that own £800 million of assets.[21] One great current example is the great British pub; the Plunkett Foundation estimates that there are 52 pubs in the UK that have been saved from closure and taken over by community groups.[22]

It doesn't just stop at individual buildings. The bigger challenge is land. Community Land Trusts are part of a longer tradition of land reform, which aims to tackle inequalities in land ownership and demonstrate that communities are the best stewards of land. Community land trusts have grown quickly across England since 2014 and there are now 160 active projects holding land and assets for the benefit of a defined community. One of the most exciting is the East London Trust, which is backed by the community organising foundation London Citizens and the city's mayor, and aims to provide 5,000 homes by 2025. Currently there are nearly 250 community land trusts across the United States, which collectively own around 10,000 homes. In Scotland, where only 16 people own 10 per cent of the country, land trusts have flourished and 500,000 acres of land are in community ownership.[23] While they are principally rural, they show what can be done, especially for urban dwellers where land is highly unequally owned. Moreover, the ENLACE community land trust in San Juan, Puerto Rico, emerged when residents were concerned that environmental improvements would lead to increased land values and hence displacement. Now residents collectively own 200 acres of land securing its use for future generations.[24] The first community land trust experiment in Africa was attempted in the Voi municipality in Kenya, which is exploring communal forms of land ownership that have not been seen since pre-colonial times. This is a genuinely worldwide movement. The International Land Coalition has over 200 members across 64 countries. Many of their initiatives focus on repopulation and renewal, which is particularly important given the problems locked into rapid peri-urban growth in mega cities.

The inner city ethnically diverse Granby area of Liverpool in northern England has become the unlikely place for one of the most inspiring land trusts. During decades of decline, the Granby Residents' Association campaigned against successive regeneration schemes which relocated many residents and led to the demolition of all but four of the area's streets. With further clearances imminent, in 2010, a group of residents began planting large flower boxes, painting murals on boarded-up houses and holding a monthly street market. The Granby 4 Streets Community Land Trust formed in 2012. This enabled the trust to eventually take ownership of 13 houses and begin rebuilding their community. They secured grant funding and collaborated with housing associations, local government and architecture and design professionals. They now plan to renovate homes to high environmental standards available for affordable rent and ownership.

Liverpool is also home to the Homebaked Community Land Trust and Cooperative Bakery situated opposite Liverpool's Anfield football stadium. The project, co-owned and co-produced by people who live and work in the area, started out by saving a local neighbourhood bakery from demolition and developed it into a thriving community-run business. Not stopping there, they aim to regenerate their high street 'brick by brick and loaf by loaf', using money that is spent in the neighbourhood to benefit the community. In my own city, I helped set up one particular land trust called Leeds Community Homes, which now runs an enabler hub to support developers, local authorities and citizens to build affordable, ecological community-led housing.

People Powered Housing

Drawing on these ideas, novel approaches to community-led house building are flourishing. For example, Zurich in Switzerland has a strong cooperative housing culture but low construction rates which has meant prices remain unaffordable for many. A 2011 referendum to increase non-profit housing allowed the 'More Than Housing' project to access a four-hectare plot of waste ground in the Hunziker Areal area of the city. Because it was an undesirable location, a consortium of more than 30 cooperatives formed to develop the project together and spread the risk. The project was conceived as a test bed for Zurich's 2,000-Watt Society model, based on reducing average energy consumption from 5,000 to 2,000 watts per person. Participatory design processes included input from prospective residents, neighbours, architectural firms, local authorities, and community groups. More Than Housing's buildings include free common areas and retail spaces, creating 150 jobs on site. Its 1,200 residents contribute to a community fund, which supports activities such as gardening, exercise and markets. Design features support low energy, heating and car use to reduce carbon emissions. Rents are set at 20 to 30 per cent below market levels, with subsidised rent for the 20 per cent of households who have below-poverty-level incomes. As one of Europe's largest-scale cooperatives, ongoing evaluations aim to identify transferable practices for other similar projects. More Than Housing has triggered a wave of sustainable housing development across Zurich. Moreover, in the city of Deventer in east Netherlands, many of the negative issues associated with ageing are being locked down through an innovative intergenerational solution. The Humanitas retirement home offers rent-free apartments to local university students, in exchange for 30 hours a month of 'neighbourliness' to the elderly residents of the home.[25]

Further, the cohousing movement has emerged over the last few decades to build gregarious and intentional communities that maximise interaction and mutual association between neighbours. The cohousing movement has its origins in Scandinavia in the 1960s. There are hundreds of cohousing projects in Denmark, which is commonly understood as the birthplace of the cohousing movement, around 300 in the Netherlands and over 100 in North America. According to the UK Cohousing Network, in 2013, there were 16 cohousing communities in the UK, with 45 in development. Smaller numbers also exist in Australia, New Zealand, Germany, France and in Scandinavian countries.[26]

The evolution of cohousing has taken different paths. The early Scandinavian examples were based on highly egalitarian values, and grew to a considerable proportion of national housing stock. North American cohousing communities flourished over the 1990s and were part of a distinctive new 'urbanist approach' to downtown renewal, which responded to the excesses of American urban blight, sprawl and the dominance of cars by introducing more people centred and fine-grained approaches to urban design. This movement has been one of my own inspirations. Over the last decade, I helped to co-found and build a cohousing cooperative called LILAC in Leeds where I now live. LILAC means Low Impact Living Affordable Community and we used that name to foreground the need to build places based on economic equality, social justice and ecological sustainability.[27]

Through my experiences with LILAC, I have been fortunate enough to encounter many amazing projects. In Northern Ireland, The Holding Project (THP) sees housing as containing the potential to unlock social mobility and change public opinion on how we live in a shared society. THP seeks to build 20 compact, eco-friendly micro-homes in Belfast for young people. As this millennial generation become trapped in private rented accommodation, the project aims to offer alternative forms of housing that can offer sociality and interaction amongst young professionals. Using vacant sites across Belfast, it aims to bring new forms of social relationships into spaces previously neglected due to the city's historical troubles.

Similarly, in suburban Amsterdam, a project called Startblok Rieker-haven responds to the city's crippling housing crisis that is hitting young people particularly hard. This is a housing project for young people aged between 18 and 28, who earn less than £30,000 a year. Homes are made from reconditioned wood and now house nearly 600 people.[28] In Sheffield in the UK, the innovator Jon Johnson set up Reach Homes to shake up the housing market. Reach takes shipping containers, combines them with other reclaimed and recycled materials, solar and ventilation systems to create energy-efficient, comfortable and secure living spaces that are built off-site and virtually zero waste, and substantially under half the price of a typical one-bedroom apartment.

In the south-west of England, in Bristol's overheated housing market, We Can Make is a live research and development programme which includes local people, architects, artists, policy makers, academics and industry professionals involved in developing ways in which citizens can have a greater role in making new homes. We Can Make focuses on reimagining the wider legal, financial and policy-enabling framework so that citizens and communities can better meet their own housing needs, rather than relying on speculative developers or top-down projects.[29] They are focusing on infill developments in deprived communities rather than new build schemes, which more directly respond to actual housing need where it exists.

The cooperative movement is a key player in building this housing common. At its most basic level, a cooperative is an autonomous association of persons who voluntarily cooperate for their mutual, social, economic and cultural benefit. Housing cooperatives are important as they foreground direct democracy through the principle of one member, one vote, and the democratic control of organisations by the people they serve. Mutual and cooperative housing solutions that have attempted to rethink housing have come in many forms: tenant management organisations, shared and part equity schemes, community gateway projects, community land trusts and short life and fully mutual housing cooperatives. However, the extent of cooperative housing is very patchy. Taking Europe as an example, in Sweden, the Czech Republic and Poland, it accounts for around 20 per cent of housing and almost 10 per cent in Denmark, but in most other countries, it accounts for a tiny or negligible amount.[30] What is clear is that there is a huge potential for the growth of mutual and self-managed housing.

Self-building has also become a new watchword to tame the power of corporate volume house builders. Self-builders have been part of the largely invisible housing revolution for decades. In the global South, most dwellings in informal settlements are built by new arrivals. In Mexico City, one estimate suggests that 60 per cent of housing is provided in that way.[31] In Europe, backed up by locally based highly skilled trades, many countries in Europe have very high levels of self-built homes. In Austria, 80 per cent of homes are self-built, while in Germany, France and Italy the figure is 60 per cent, and in the USA and Australia, it is over 40 per cent.[32] Custom-build has entered into the lexicon alongside self-build. Small-scale innovative builders using modern methods of construction can offer individuals and groups the opportunity to design and customise their own homes.

Not surprisingly, it is the Dutch that are leading the way. In Almere, one of the fastest growing cities in Europe, 100 hectares of land reclaimed from the sea has been devoted to the world's largest custom-build experiment. The entire area has been master planned into districts where 3,000 self-built homes are planned. To date, about one-third of this has been completed. In the UK, the National Custom and Self Build Association (NaCSBA) was set up to try and increase the share of homes provided through self- and custom-build routes, which is languishing at around 10 per cent of all new homes. The UK Government has set ambitious targets to double the size of this sector over the next decade from 100,000 to 200,000.[33] Collective custom-build is fast taking off, where groups can come together to buy plots or part-finished buildings. The UK's first Plot Shop has officially opened in Bicester. Right on the high street, it sells plots of land at a nearby site for those wishing to build their own home from scratch or through customised design. Once finished, it will be the largest of its kind in the UK, aiming to deliver nearly 2,000 new self- and custom-build homes.[34]

Key to unlocking this community housing common is better information, especially in terms of who owns land. In the UK, DemoDev is working with the Land Registry and the national mapping agency Ordnance Survey in collaboration with Birmingham City Council to unlock underused land and turn it into open designed, sustainable, adaptable homes. Their aim is to help build a movement that enables a new sector of citizen builders to create homes which are in areas people want to live in, which can be self-built and can grow and change as their owner's lives evolve.[35] DemoDev draws on the WikiHouse approach, an open-source project to reinvent the way homes are made. WikiHouse is being developed by architects, designers, engineers, inventors, manufacturers and builders, collaborating to develop simple, sustainable, high-performance building technologies, which anyone can use and improve. The aim is for these technologies to become new industry standards; the bricks and mortar of the digital age is the WikiHouse motto.

Of course, given the power and entrenchment of the neoliberal housing model, more direct interventions as well as citizen direct action will be needed to unlock the potential of the urban common. In Barcelona, for example, the Platform For Mortgage Victims (PAH) championed the rights of those not able to pay their mortgages or who were facing eviction. PAH was so successful it created a new citizens' movement, Barcelona en Comú. On the back of these successes, one of the organisers, Ada Colau, was elected city mayor in 2015, and has become part of a new breed of radical mayors standing up to the excesses of the neoliberal urban growth machine. Meanwhile, the London Renters Union was set up in 2017 in the face of the chronic shortage of affordable homes in the UK capital. By 2025, most Londoners will be private renters, and in this context, the group aims to proliferate renters unions across the city to organise and demand housing justice. In the USA, the Right To The City Alliance emerged in 2007 as a response to gentrification and a call to halt the displacement of low-income groups, people of colour and marginalised communities. It now has dozens of chapter organisations across the USA. And in the global South, there are more dramatic flashpoints of struggles to defend and reclaim the urban common. In South Africa, where 10 per cent of people live in shack developments, Abahlali baseMjondolo (The Shack Dwellers Movement), has been taking action and campaigning against evictions and for public housing. And in Brazil, the Movimento Dos Trabalhadores Sem Teto (The Homeless Workers Movement) has been taking direct action over the last two decades to confront the drastic inequalities in land ownership, most successfully by squatting abandoned land and buildings in Brazilian cities.

Retrofitting the Corporate City

The urban common requires a new urban economy. Given that the capitalist economy isn't going to disappear anytime soon, building the common city also requires retrofitting the corporate city and unleashing the potential of a common economy. This entails a radical reskilling around green sectors, new civic institutions to retain, build and circulate wealth, collaborative production, local currencies and citizen and micro-civic finance. This community economy is based on radically different principles that counter the individualism, competition and private profit of the business-as-usual economic machine. It values economic resilience, self-provisioning, community wealth building, solidarity and reciprocity, and creating abundance rather than scarcity. Unlocking this other economy requires broad action including a new institutional basis for educational, financial and trading institutions, as well as differently crafted places for consumption and production.

The push for a new economy is far from new. The 1960s and 1970s brought crisis in the post-war economy and a growing awareness that something was deeply flawed with the high growth model being pushed by the advanced economies of the global North. A whole generation of radical and ecologically inspired economic thinking from E.F. Schumacher to Herman Daly and Richard Douthwaite, has now converged into what is called post-growth economics.[36] It elaborates a simple message – the illusion, and dangers, of infinite economic growth on an ecologically finite planet.[37] But this is not an anti-development agenda. As Tim Jackson, Professor of Sustainable Development argues, the challenge is to establish a new basis for prosperity without ceaseless economic growth.[38] Greening the growth machine and decarbonising economic output is central here. The urgent first step is to unlock economic output as far as possible from carbon emissions. Developing infrastructure for a new green economy in renewable technologies, low-carbon housing or the electrification of urban mobility, as well as the skills that underpin them will certainly reconfigure our economies. Millions of new green jobs can be unlocked as the brown fossil fuel dependent economy is locked down.[39] But urban economic retrofitting needs to go much further. The more difficult step is to reduce the drive towards overall levels of economic growth and consumerism. Here, we enter into the terrain of anti-capitalist, or post-capitalist, economics based around socially useful production and reconfiguring the very nature of work, property and class relations.[40]

The 2008 global crisis as well as the continuing breakdown of the global climate brought these issues into stark relief. They raised the prospect for a new global economic deal which would radically depart from the casino-like global free market capitalist economy. The sociologist Juliet

Schor calls this Plenitude,[41] how we can forge an economy based on a new deal that can balance the needs of the global biosphere and its inhabitants. Similarly, Kate Raworth has crystallised this as humanity's twenty-first century challenge; how to meet the needs of all while ensuring that collectively we do not overshoot Earth's life-supporting systems on which we fundamentally depend.[42] She stresses the need to rebuild economies in ways that are both regenerative and distributive, echoing permaculture's triad of principles: people care, fair shares and earth care. In contrast to the current linear model of relying on high throughputs of large quantities of cheap, easily accessible materials and energy, city economic retrofitting creates a circular economy. This kind of economy is restorative and regenerative by design, rather than treating natural capital as a free external input. It preserves and enhances them and foregrounds our interconnectedness with them. Underpinning all these is a fundamentally different model for measuring progress. Measurements such as Gross Domestic Product (GDP) are so ingrained as to be unquestioned as benchmarks of what we value. But several other measurements exist such as the Index of Sustainable Economic Welfare (ISEW) and the Genuine Progress Indicator.[43] Rather than simply adding together all expenditures within a territory, this is balanced with considerations such as income distribution, costs of pollution, environmental degradation and the depreciation of natural capital, as well as positively accounting for social value through parenting and volunteering. At the city level, The Happy City Index was developed by Bristol-based Happy City and think-tank New Economics Foundation to monitor city progress towards providing the conditions that create well-being in a fair and sustainable way. It has begun a process of scoring cities using 60 indicators with the likes of Bristol and Leeds scoring higher than Manchester and Liverpool.[44]

Understanding this task of retrofitting the corporate city economy is well underway. Scholars in the Community Economies Research Network, building on the foundational work of inspirational writing team J.K. Gibson-Graham, have provided a detailed understanding of how to create a less capital-centric economy.[45] They have stressed that the economy has always been made up of diverse components. The mainstream, pro-growth capitalist economy, while it gets a lot of airtime, is in fact only the tip of the economic iceberg. Below the water, there has always been the invisible economic bedrock taken up by, for example, community economic activity, household labour, cooperatives and free exchange. These are the aspects that provide flourishing and well-being at a local level. They provide the ingredients for a positive upward spiral of growth between community wealth building institutions. Researchers from the Centre for Research on Socio-Cultural Change at Manchester University in the UK have called this the foundational economy – the mundane yet vital areas of the economy that provide the goods and services essential for citizens' well-being including infrastructures, utilities, food, retailing and distribution, health, education and welfare.[46] Equally, the Democracy Collaborative in the USA has outlined a vision of a new economic system, where shared ownership and control creates more equitable and inclusive outcomes including ecological sustainability and flourishing democratic and community life. One of their offshoot projects is the Next System Project. It aims to promote visions, models and pathways that point to a next system radically different in fundamental ways from the failed systems of the past and present.[47]

So what are the essential ingredients of this new urban economy? Cooperatives have long played a key role in community wealth building. The cooperative movement emerged from the early decades of the Industrial Revolution in northern England where workers associated and organised for their survival and common good. The first formal cooperative is usually claimed to be the Rochdale Society of Equitable Pioneers, founded amongst the weavers and artisans of Lancashire in 1844. The second half of the nineteenth century saw the cooperative movement flourish through the growth of friendly societies and consumer cooperatives. From these humble and radical origins, the cooperative sector now forms a fairly significant part of the economy. Worker, producer and consumer cooperatives have focused on generating and retaining wealth for the benefit of their members and the wider community. There are now more than 1 billion members of cooperatives worldwide, which employ over 100 million people and have a turnover of $1.1 trillion dollars. In the UK alone, cooperatives have a combined turnover of more than £35.6 billion and are owned by 13.5 million people.[48]

One of the most inspiring examples still remains the Mondragon Corporation, a federation of worker cooperatives in the Basque region of Spain. Founded in 1956, it is now the tenth-largest Spanish company and employs around 75,000 people across finance, industry, retail and knowledge sectors.[49] Throughout the world, cooperatives are recognised as key elements of creating community wealth. The Evergreen Cooperative Initiative is behind what is dubbed the Cleveland Model, an experiment in alternative wealth building and wealth sharing, where stakeholders come together to create local economic development, green job creation and neighbourhood stabilisation. The model is based on the creation of large-scale community enterprises, part-owned by their employees. It is now being taken seriously by municipalities across the world to stop cycles of urban decline, unemployment and disinvestment.

Moreover, The Cooperativa Integral Catalana or CIC (Catalan Integrated Cooperative) began as a small cooperative in 2008 and became a larger integrated network in 2010. It now has 850 members participating in various autonomous initiatives such as housing, transport and health care. CIC participants meet in open assemblies fortnightly to make decisions about the cooperative's general functioning, and local nodes or hubs deal with particular aspects of the organisation such as communication, legal structure and supply infrastructure.

The key aspect for CIC is that it is much more than a consumer cooperative. Members also participate in education, a cooperative basic income platform, collective eco-stores, meetings and events. The CIC's general principles focus on social transformation, equality in society, a needs-focused economy, ecological responsibility, transparency, decentralised self-management and collective decision-making. CIC is part of a booming solidarity economy across the region. The Catalan Solidarity Economy Network has 190 member organisations with a combined turnover of €165 million and employs 4,000 people across a range of sectors.[50] It is also part of a national network of regional integrated cooperatives.

Meanwhile, in Jackson, Mississippi, one of the poorest cities in the USA where the population is 80 per cent black and mostly working class, unmet social and economic needs are high. This is exacerbated by disinvestment, deindustrialisation and suburban flight. The Cooperation Jackson initiative emerged from this context. It sees a cooperative economy as the best way to address these unmet needs, because this approach puts work, wealth and decision-making in the hands of the people who buy and sell goods and services. Cooperation Jackson aims to create, over the coming years and decades, a cooperative network to empower and meet the needs of local residents. Its overarching vision encompasses a federation of cooperative enterprises, an incubator for developing new cooperatives and a training and education centre. The first generation of enterprises includes a cooperative farm, café and catering cooperative, a recycling and composting firm, community land trust, and community production internships in sustainable digital manufacturing.[51]

Alternative ways of using and exchanging money are growing. Complementary and community currencies put alternative money systems into the local economy that can be used alongside national currencies.[52] The Complementary Currency Resource Centre estimates that there are 4,500 local currencies worldwide. Time Banking has also emerged as a way to facilitate reciprocal service exchange that uses units of time as currency. Early pioneering examples included the Ithaca Hour, a local currency used in Ithaca, New York, which is the oldest and largest local currency system in the United States. Members trade Hour notes, worth $10 dollars (pegged at the local minimum wage) via a directory, which lists services on offer.[53] In the UK, there are over 400 local exchange trading systems (LETS), nearly 100 time banks and a handful of functioning local currencies in places such as Brixton, Totnes, Lewes and Cardiff.[54]

Brixton was the first to launch a complementary currency in a UK city. With its motto 'Money That Sticks To Brixton', the Brixton pound (B£) was launched as a paper currency in 2009, and in 2011 as a digital currency with a pay-by-text system. The Brixton Pound Shop and Café provide an administrative hub and community space. Individuals and businesses can open electronic accounts, and over 250 businesses in Brixton accept payment in B£. Businesses can pay rates to Lambeth Council in B£ and can offer B£ as a proportion of salaries to employees. Business members pay a 1.5 per cent transaction fee on B£ transactions. Surplus revenue goes into the Brixton Pound Fund, which provides micro-grants to community initiatives.[55] The key aspect of all these alternative economic experiments is that they directly tie money to a particular locality, slowing down the external leaking of wealth.

More profoundly, there are attempts to reconfigure work and the local welfare state. The Basic or Citizen's Income is an idea that is coming of age. Under such proposals, citizens receive a regular unconditional sum of money paid from reallocating money previously paid through the social security and welfare systems. Advocates say it will allow people to genuinely choose what sort of employment they take, and to retrain when they wish, and for this reason it has also been given the name Citizen's Wage. The Scottish Government is investigating the practicalities of such an approach in the wake of the Glasgow City Council commissioning a feasibility study for its own basic income pilot. Further, the Finnish government recently undertook a trial involving 2,000 people over two years and several Dutch cities including Leiden have trialled it amongst welfare recipients.[56]

Finally, central to this common urban economy are workers who have taken back control of their workplaces, literally taking back the means of production through workplace recuperations. In the wake of various crises over the couple of decades, Latin America has been a hotspot for these. By early 2016, there were approximately 360 recuperated workplaces in Argentina, involving 15,000 workers, and around 80 in Brazil employing 12,000.[57] These recuperated workplaces become democratically self-managed micro-communities many of which are thriving, such as the Brukman textile factory now run by the *18 of December* workers cooperative. A broader infrastructure has developed to sell goods from these recuperated factories in worker-controlled supermarkets, street markets, barter networks and even online platforms. This is part of a wider growth of a solidarity economy where social movements and a radicalised civil society play a central role in reorientating the economy towards social ends.[58]

Relearning Civic Democracy

The final piece of the puzzle is the health of local civic democracy. The urban common cannot flourish without the equal participation and representation of urban residents. As John Alexander of the New Citizen Project notes, while the twentieth century was the age of the subject and the early twenty-first century is the age of the consumer, we may be in transition to the age of the citizen where we recognise our interdependence and collectively deliberate on the challenges ahead.[59] I would push this further and say that we urgently need the age of the urban commoner. Clearly, there are huge obstacles here not least the need for education, inequality of access to resources, the need for greater time, as well as experiences of direct oppression and surveillance amongst those attempting to reconfigure urban democracy.

The late Colin Ward, inspirational and tireless advocate for an anarchist social policy stated that the city is a public good and the common property of its inhabitants.[60] In this sense, the city is a common that is governed by and for its citizens to maximise internal democracy, well-being and flourishing. This does not just involve land and assets, but also governance arrangements. One of his enduring insights is that policy and management options cannot be known or determined in advance of a commitment to participation.

Building the urban common requires going beyond familiar forms of representative democracy and vastly increasing participation in decision-making. It requires what Benjamin Barber called strong forms of democracy, which will allow mutuality, horizontality, self-management and autonomy to flourish.[61] Rather than casting them as villains, city authorities become enablers in this great unleashing of urban democratic potential, facilitating and enabling popular assemblies, participatory budgets, citizen's forums, distributed networks, co-production methodologies and cooperatives. The crucial aspect is addressing the power inequalities and restoring balance between civil society, public and private sector partners; ensuring genuine democratic mechanisms not just for debate, but for agenda setting, budgetary control and accountability between different sectors. Digital tools, from crowdsourcing and collaborative policy-making to large-scale deliberative exercises, are transforming civic politics, making it possible to connect and engage citizens in new ways to solve complex problems.

A handful of cities have taken this agenda seriously. Some have begun crowdsourcing future policy ideas and directions from their citizens. Mexico City is using an innovative digital platform to crowdsource responses to a new city constitution that has been drafted by a group of 30 experts. Just before the 2017 mayoral elections in the West Midlands and Greater Manchester regions in the UK, the People's Plan was launched by a coalition of civic activists to crowdsource ideas to influence this new post. The ideas were sorted with draft action plans created for each and then put to the new mayor.[62] In Iceland, Better Reykjavík is an online consultation forum where citizens can present their ideas for the running of the city. The municipality commits itself to formally addressing the five top-rated ideas in the appropriate standing committee every month. To date, over 17,000 users have submitted more than 6,000 ideas.[63]

Moreover, from its origins in Porto Alegre in Brazil, participatory budgeting continues to take hold in localities across the world, with an estimated 1,500 localities taking part. It is a democratic process in which urban residents directly decide how to spend part of the municipal budget. In North America, the Participatory Budgeting Project has engaged 300,000 people across 22 cities to decide how to spend $238 million.[64] Paris aims to spend €500 million through its programme by

2020, and in 2016, Portugal announced the world's first participatory budget on a national scale.[65]

As well as specific projects, a new sensibility is required. Urban democratic renewal entails a commitment to co-producing city futures. Co-production is a particularly useful methodology for addressing fragmentation and disengagement through overcoming silo working practices, making connections across institutions and in an urban context, generating better outcomes for citizens. It attempts to harness co-working and co-design aimed at collaborative problem-solving embedded in a commitment to mutual respect, equality and developing shared learning. By creating greater co-ownership of problems, co-production can generate a wider range of more creative and durable solutions to persistent problems.

Co-production spaces continue to proliferate through various guises: innovation labs, urban labs and city rooms for example. They are part of a new way of producing knowledge, which is cyclical and interdisciplinary, compared to previous models based on disciplinary silos or lone scholars and charismatic entrepreneurs. These urban labs are part of a desire to create places for convergence amongst urban innovators. They are places of assembly which are as ancient as the Agora of Athens and have continued across the ages in various guises. Ray Oldenburg called these the Great Good Place, those essential community settings where people assemble and interact and include cafés, coffee shops, bookstores, bars, hair salons, working men's clubs and community centres.[66]

Across the world, urban labs have appeared to harness this new democratic impulse and tackle urban challenges. For example, MIT's (Massachusetts Institute for Technology) Civic Data Design Lab and the Co-Creation Hub in Nigeria bring together digital entrepreneurs, UCHICAGO Urban Lab and the SENSEable City Laboratory at MIT study urban changes and make interventions to prompt progressive outcomes. Fab Labs have also spread rapidly into a global network of small-scale local workshops, enabling invention by providing access to tools for digital fabrication. Birmingham's Impact Hub sees its role as part of reinventing civic democracy. It describes itself as a welcoming and malleable space where eclectic individuals can collaborate to tackle some of the most pressing problems of the city. For Hub users, organising around a single discipline would only increase the silo effect in the city and structurally lock out solutions that address the interdependent problems that affect us all. They see their wider mission as prototyping the twenty-first century town hall. Play can perform a vital role in these new forms of democratic engagement. For example, the organisation CounterPlay undertakes an annual festival to show how play and playful activities can change our relationship to each other, our public spaces and ourselves.

Moreover, the Office for Civic Imagination in Bologna, Italy, is a policy innovation lab which encourages co-working between local civil servants where they can work together to find innovative solutions to common problems and implement civic collaboration. One of their tasks is to evaluate processes and policies in the city to better understand their impact on urban democracy. These initiatives have networked to increase their impact. For example, the 170-member European Network of Living Labs is a user-centred, open innovation ecosystem based on a co-creation approach in real life settings.[67]

And this is also being rolled out at a larger scale. The Participatory City Foundation began the Every One Every Day initiative in the London borough of Barking and Dagenham in 2017. Every One Every Day is a growing network of neighbourhood initiatives and businesses that combine peer-to-peer co-production projects that work together to improve the overall well-being of all neighbourhood residents. Every One Every Day invites people to suggest ideas for projects and businesses they would like to create together, providing the support needed to bring hundreds of these ideas to life quickly and without complicated processes. It is already opening high street shops and a central warehouse where a team will work with people to create projects, arrange insurances and health and safety, set up websites, produce newspapers, hold festivals, workshops and business development incubator programmes.[68]

A new approach to education underpins this democratic renewal. Drawing on radical education activists Paulo Freire and Myles Horton, the tradition of popular education has long been used as a tool for raising consciousness, building solidarity and empowerment, developing grounded social critique and proposing empowering alternatives.[69] Storytelling and narrating future possibilities for change are important here, especially in terms of reviving folk and vernacular knowledges and customs, challenging powerlessness in the face of capitalism and harnessing the power of positive change stories. The Transition Towns movement calls this the great reskilling, where interpersonal, democratic, communicative and emotional abilities are relearned to nurture more collective subjectivities.

Specific approaches can also enhance deliberative and deeper forms of decision-making between individuals. For example, non-violent communication (NVC) is a technique developed by Marshall Rosenberg, an American psychologist and founder of the Centre for Nonviolent Communication in the 1960s.[70] NVC is a conflict resolution process, which aims to improve three aspects of how we communicate: self-empathy, which is about tuning into one's own experience; empathy, which focuses on listening to others drawing on a compassionate approach; and self-expression, which attempts to allow individuals to express themselves authentically to inspire compassion in others. NVC is a hopeful approach that assumes all of us have the capacity for compassion. It helps people identify established patterns of thinking and speaking that lead to communicative violence. NVC proposes that if people can identify their needs, and those of others, less conflictual ways of communication can be achieved. This is a crucial task given the complexities and divergences locked up in managing modern cities.

Moreover, consensus-based decision-making can enhance deliberative democracy. It is used in small and large group contexts where participants can agree proposals in a dialogue between equals. A number of deliberative steps are used such as discussion events, working groups, templates for proposals and training facilitators to ensure that decisions are not rushed, and that outcomes can be owned by everyone. What consensus tries to do is unlock whole group decision-making. Moreover, holistic approaches such as Sociocracy and Holacracy have been developed to govern organisations and groups in more horizontal ways, to create distributed forms of leadership as well as greater creativity, productivity and contentment.[71] A handful of organisations around the world use these methods ranging from housing cooperatives to schools and mental healthcare providers.

Extra parliamentary activities, civil disobedience and direct action also play a vital role as an important check on creeping authoritarianism and unjust laws. History teaches us that the common has to be defended. The planet is riven by struggles to defend it; the land occupations of the Movement of Landless Workers in Brazil, the Zapatista Autonomous Municipalities of Chiapas, Mexico, the South African Shack Dwellers Movement, the Bangladesh Krishok Federation (BKF), the anti-fracking and anti-fossil fuel movements, the central encampments in the wake of the Arab Spring and the Occupy movement, and more recent anti-austerity groups such as the People's Assembly Against

Austerity. Moreover, struggles to create the urban common are evident in a multitude of small moments of guerrilla or tactical urbanism, encompassing micro interventions such as urban gardening, street art, road blocks, civic demonstrations, subvertising or adbusting corporate billboards, as well as more mundane everyday acts of kindness, social care and togetherness that form the basis for how commoners can enact the urban common in their everyday lives. Independent social centres have emerged from this impulse in many cities across the world to radicalise civil society. In the UK, for example, during the early 2000s, a network of 14 social centres were established to specifically explore how neighbourhood spaces could act as hubs for social activism, solidarity and community self-management, featuring aspects such as pay as you feel kitchens, do it yourself workshops and meeting spaces.[72] They built upon the longer traditions of the Italian centri sociali and German and Dutch squatting movements. This tradition continues and responds to many contemporary crises. For example, in Greece's capital, Athens, a cooperatively run community centre, Khora has been set up for migrants and refugees who have arrived in the city with no clear idea of what the future holds. Set up in 2016 and run by volunteers, its ethos is that everyone should have freedom of movement and that people can develop and share skills, and feel a sense of belonging, self-worth and respect as part of a diverse and welcoming community. Free classes and services include childcare and meals, language lessons, legal advice, women's space, a café and workshop.[73]

These kinds of projects highlight injustices, defend social wealth, collectively organise to challenge resource dispossessions and help imagine alternatives. Their potential is to unlock the collective power of marginalised groups so they can mount a connected challenge to the present balance of power away from coalitions of multinational institutions towards a globally connected grass-roots movement. At their best, they are transformative and prefigurative of possible, but as yet unknown, sustainable cities.

*   *   *

This is the broad ranging and complex challenge of the common city. Given the uncommon, corporate nature of our contemporary urban world, many of these examples may well remain defiant markers waiting for, and signalling, better times ahead. The challenge, as always, remains to strategically reflect on what this means. How do micro-examples connect and scale without losing their potency? How do we embed social justice in sustainable cities? How do we ensure that common building blocks are inclusive and representative of diverse voices? What coalitions of actors will move us in these directions? I now turn to these issues in the conclusion.

5

Think Big, Act Small, Start Now

So what kind of real change does this add up to? What is the scale of the task? Is it already too late? Do we actually have the skills, resources, capabilities and insights to overcome the multiple challenges we face? Can a new relationship be brokered between state, market and civil society? These are the questions that we need to have some responses to. To conclude this journey through unlocking sustainable cities, I want to offer some strategic reflections on issues of organisation and questions of geography and scale.

I frame this chapter with the phrase, think big, act small, start now. First, we have to think big. Given the challenges ahead this is an agenda for real and substantive urban transformation, a purposeful step change away from the status quo. We have to do different things and do them differently across a whole range of areas: politics, culture, commerce, work, travel. Second, we have to break this down into manageable chunks and simply try things out on a small scale. There is no workable blueprint for unlocking sustainable urban futures that can be rolled out. Given the complexity of the modern metropolis, we simply cannot predict what will work or offer the kinds of outcomes we require. As MIT's SENSEable City Lab team point out, it's more likely to emerge from throwing out experimental mutations into the urban realm, testing, evaluating and prototyping the future.[1] As I explore below, this is not anti-organising. It's a radically different approach to organising the future sustainable city. Finally, we have to start now. Every generation feels an urgency and that their time has come. Our generation feels this acutely, motivated by a now-or-never mentality. Given the warning shots being fired by the scientific community on a range of issues including biodiversity loss, water stress, food loss, extreme weather and climate breakdown, as well as the mounting number of early indicators the global biosphere is offering us, I suggest that the precautionary principle is a smart approach.

ORGANISING SUSTAINABLE URBAN FUTURES

Significant debates rage in terms of how, whether, and indeed, if it even makes sense to try and organise the future. Amongst the incredible levels of global uncertainty, scenario planning and creating transition pathways and road maps for the future have become big business. Groups as disparate as the UK Government's Foresight Programme, Permaculture activists and global consultants have attempted to develop and predict options ranging from future collapse, radical transformation, business-as-usual, as well as technocratic-led renewal. There are certainly some dramatic choices here. The key question is under what conditions will the kinds of examples presented in this book flourish. In the Introduction, I pointed to some of the essential ingredients: compassion, imagination, experimentation, co-production and transformation. And while this might not explicitly be an anti-capitalist, or a post-capitalist, agenda, the sum of all these efforts might lead that way. In this context, it is worth clarifying what exactly I am advocating for.

I am not proposing a meta-narrative or a unified strategy about how the future could or should unfold. Indeed, the recent work of both Erik Olin Wright and John Holloway helps us see that change in our connected and complex world will come through multiple and simultaneous strategic approaches.[2] There are those who will pursue more radical and ruptural approaches, agitating against the current state and market relations to usher in a radically different social deal. Similarly, there are those who will seek more reformist and gradualist change working symbiotically inside existing structures, while taking a longer and incrementalist view, building competences in the here and now to leverage social change. And others, perhaps more utopian or intentional, will attempt to opt out on the basis of principle or frustration, creating what is called interstitial or prefigurative examples of the future in the present.[3] These latter forms are particularly important, providing 'research and development' prototypes that we can assess in terms of what tangible results future configurations offer. And this will also include disruptive and disobedient actions, which highlight injustice and protect the rights of marginalised groups.

The key point for organising sustainable urban futures is that these are not mutually exclusive. In particular, the most productive breakthroughs will come from combining these approaches. Localised projects will need a radical enabling state in order to flourish, as well as active social movements, pushing the boundaries of what is possible. Reclaiming the state towards progressive ends remains a crucial task. We are seeing glimpses of this through a revival of Marxist ideas in the wake of the post-2008 crash and experiments with popular left movements such as Podemos in Spain and Syriza in Greece, as well as the previous wave of radical leaders during Latin America's Pink Tide. And recent experiments around Jeremy Corbyn and Bernie Saunders show what can be achieved when a radical social organising mentality is re-energised in big politics.[4] So-called 'accelerationists', an emerging movement of thinkers and activists, offer some exciting insights here. They see a new political project based on accelerating technology and vast state resources to maximise the benefits of a more complex society. From this perspective, the current version of big monopolistic capitalism is anti-modern, holding back the kind of social progress that we could make. Trends such as automated work, citizen incomes and local digital currencies show ways to reclaim left modernity through repurposing technology and the big state towards common sustainable and equitable ends.[5] Clearly there are some significant caveats here that need to be closely managed, especially in terms of a naive faith in the ability to harness new technologies and government apparatus to progressive ends.

Nevertheless, at the city level, there is an emerging project of radical municipalism. We need a new generation of civic leaders who are prepared to break from the status quo of big business, top-down politics, the corporate university and a withered civil society. This radical municipalism might be the key to the twin dynamics of unlocking and lock-down that frames this book. New legislation and brave decisions will be needed from municipal leaders to constrain and curtail damaging activities. They will also have a role in setting transformative agendas and visions, but in ways that embed radically new forms of citizen democracy and participation. Equally, state resources need to be unleashed to enable and facilitate these radical projects, many of which will wither without support and protection. Municipal resources and legislation need to systematically hold back corporate power and at the same time nurture those social innovators and associated resources in their efforts to super-charge civic energy, nature-based solutions, common infrastructure and car-free activities.

There is also the issue of harnessing the potential of the four big city sectors equally: commerce, the state, civil society and the academy. Those localities that are able to rise to future challenges unlock the power of cross-sector place leadership, bringing together these sectors in ways that address historic power imbalances. In sum, there needs to be a new configuration and social deal between city sectors playing powerful, distinct and complementary roles: a radical, participatory and enabling state at the local and national level which also returns to its historic welfarist role, an energised and strengthened civil society, a responsible and civic-minded corporate sector, a supported constellation of social entrepreneurs and businesses, and a locally engaged, independent and creative academy.

This new configuration can rise to the great unlocking challenge through new civic institutional and governance arrangements that avoid workplace silos and traditional left–right dichotomies. An urgent organisational challenge for municipalities is to support novel meso-level institutions that can incorporate diverse voices as well as enabling and protecting projects as they emerge. These kinds of entities are populated by disruptive social innovators, who scale upwards seeking influence amongst more powerful institutions as well as reaching outwards to multiple projects at the grass-roots level. Moreover, transformative places embrace collaborative forms of leadership and competencies in co-production. They are led by teams who are comfortable with working between and across sectors and harnessing interdisciplinary knowledge. One of the particularly useful tendencies that needs to be further encouraged is the blurring of boundaries between the social entrepreneur and the social activist. Those innovators who can adopt a social movement mindset to change, while also developing an entrepreneurial mentality to financial planning will be able to unlock serious potential. Interventions need to challenge the corporate growth machine but they also ultimately need to be feasible and durable. As we saw earlier in the book, this is about unlocking the growth dynamic of the common economy around worker cooperatives and community businesses that can build and retain local common wealth.

Much of the great unlocking process is wishful thinking, without significant resources and a productive relationship with regional and central tiers of government.[6] Municipalities need to find localised ways to generate working capital to begin the great unlocking. Local bonds and currencies are a step in this direction. But significant resources and primary legislation is required and existing subsidies need redeploying. Reforming the tax system, for example, through a shift from income tax to a land tax and recirculating the proceeds can help create and retain new forms of value within cities. And of course, more sinister and interventionist tendencies can also thwart radical transitioning. These can take many forms: bureaucratic stalling, the removal of municipal powers, police infiltration or, especially in the global South, military or paramilitary interventions. These are huge and ever-present dangers and there are no easy answers. A connected and empowered civil society can be more resilient in the face of such threats. Building networks of local and global solidarity can help defend and expand radical place-based projects. Non-violent communication and restorative practices can also reduce the potential of local conflicts. But the broader point is that organising sustainable urban futures will continue to be a deeply political and contentious process.

In the end, the task of trying to organise future urban sustainability can be a fool's errand. Cities are simultaneously domains of complexity, control, disorder, structure and breakdown.[7] In such a globalised and fast-paced world, it is difficult to grasp the essence of urbanity, its main actors, drivers and institutions or meaningfully locate where decisions are made. In particular, many attempts to put urban sustainability into practice lose traction on the actual scale and complexity of the fundamental causes of unsustainability: pro-growth economics, hyper-consumerism and meeting the relentless needs of a rapidly growing humanity across the globe. The unspoken challenge of sustainability is staring us in the face: to fundamentally rethink our own role as a human species, our damaging planetary effects over the last 500 years, and how we can rebalance our impacts alongside the interconnected web of other species and ecosystems.

EMERGING GEOGRAPHIES OF REAL SUSTAINABLE CITIES

Given this is a book emerging from radical geography, I want to ask what exactly is the geography of this sustainable urban future? Clearly, there is not one single locality in the world where all the approaches in this book come together. Some, perhaps Copenhagen, Mexico City, Curitiba or New York, offer broad glimpses. And there are many efforts, most as yet unfulfilled and possibly undesirable, to establish green urban utopias from scratch through new eco-cities and eco-towns, especially across China and the Middle East. But, most urban places are a patchwork of some of the best, worst and simply mundane tendencies. We have to remember, that the majority urban experience across the globe plays out in smaller cities and larger towns, those ordinary places away from the spotlight of world city innovation. For most urban dwellers, life simply proceeds as normal, with the kinds of examples in this book being rarely visible. But in many ways, this is the key to the future geography of urban sustainability. It will need to emerge from, resonate with and take hold within, the mundane and ordinary places for it to have broad impact.

One of the central challenges ahead is to develop a clear, powerful and hopeful spatial vocabulary for describing the feel and look of sustainable urban places in the coming decades. This is a tremendously difficult task given that it is almost impossible to predict the suite of options and impacts that future innovations will open up. The big unknown is the trajectory of current technological developments, and especially how integrated digital, artificial and intelligent systems will start to combine and alter our workplaces, health systems, transport modes and homes. The faith that a basket of technologies will resolve social problems will continue to loom large. And this is the dominant narrative pushed through a global smart city agenda where the Internet of Everything harnesses the potential of digital platforms to facilitate efficient and lower carbon urban living for a digital savvy citizenry. There will always be technological winners and losers. The smart city will bring all sorts of advances especially in transport, education and health. But serious questions remain over the issues of control and the distribution of benefits. While many small digital creative entrepreneurs underpin the move to the smart city, it is super-charging growth for global corporate giants such as Cisco and Siemens, who are literally laying down and taking ownership of the future digital infrastructure of cities. This is no surprise given that the smart city solutions market could be worth over $1.5 trillion in the next couple of years.[8]

Dystopian spatial visions also emerge, if we soberly extrapolate some of the current tendencies into the future. Without seriously planned interventions, immense social, digital and work divides will continue to combine and enhance in new ways, creating sharp ghettos of the haves and have-nots. These are entirely feasible, and in some parts of the world, reflect current reality. As the sci-fi writer William Gibson commented, 'the future is already here, it's just not evenly distributed'.[9] Significant political intervention will be required to arrest and reverse these tendencies. I have always found extremely useful the approach represented by the Luddites during the emergence of the Industrial Revolution in northern England: we are not against technological advancement, but technology that is hurtful to commonality. The quest, now as then, is to harness the great human impulse towards innovation and advancement, to common ends.

But it is clear that if the positive trends in this book are substantially unlocked, the everyday texture of urban areas will be drastically restructured. This will be in terms of the visible form and function of city infrastructure systems across not only transport, energy, community and work but also the profound re-workings of less visible systems around welfare, democracy, justice and education. Fundamental is locking down some of the negative spatial trends towards centralised cities, peri-urban development, suburban sprawl and megacities. This is a generational and global task and would require significant, and possibly unacceptable, realignments in population, underpinned by urban dedensification and well thought out rural repopulation programmes. The aim may be a very different urban form. Cityness will mean something quite different. There is little need to hold onto the spatial templates of the past. The post-carbon, car-free, common bio city will take its own spatial twists and turns. It is likely that sustainability gains will be maximised through a return to smaller, compact and better-connected settlements comprising layers of highly localised and interdependent zero-carbon and socially just human settlements. And connections to non-urban, rural areas will be greater. A colleague of mine calls this urbalism; the development of outside-in cities and bringing back, and making productive, the deep interconnections between the urban and the rural, perhaps to a point where the distinction between the two is blurred.[10] This is not a route to the final destruction of the countryside. It is a disruptive ontological leap into a yet largely unknown spatial form and function where there is a new human–natural deal. And there have been radical and feasible precedents here in the work of thinkers such as Patrick Geddes, Ebenezer Howard and Peter Kropotkin.[11]

The future geography of the sustainable city will also simply have to work with what already exists. Given that this is also not a manifesto for mass urban clearances, or urbicide as the urban theorist Steve Graham called it,[12] urban retrofitting becomes a central tool in the repertoire of action. Tony Fry calls this metrofitting, where the urban fabric is repaired in a way that redirects it to be able to deal with emergent conditions.[13] Actions and activities will have to interact, layer and combine with what already exists. Most cities around the world are already undertaking programmes of building work that commits them to particular pathways for the coming decades. These cannot easily be undone. The task becomes overlaying infrastructures and processes on what already exists. Repurposing will be central – taking what is already there and setting it to a new task. Clearly, this repurposing agenda can be super-charged in cities that can lay down a strategic enabling framework. Equally, at every step, broad deliberation is required over the impact and likely outcomes of significant options. Some might lock cities into weak gains. Others might offer unanticipated co-benefits or indeed negative and perverse outcomes. The most productive will be those that offer gains across multiple city systems: road closures repurposed for food growing, rewilding to increase flood resilience, housing retrofits that generate local green energy.

What are some steps to work towards this? The examples in this book are archipelagos of innovation. As we have seen, they don't all exist in the same localities. They are a largely non-contiguous constellation of projects, ideas and people. But they are still strongly connected through relatively instantaneous and diffuse networks of learning and exchange that span the globe. Conceived as such, we are facing a web of innovation more redolent of the rhizomatic structures discussed by the French post-structural philosophers Deleuze and Guattari.[14] What they found was the potential of unregulated, non-hierarchical networks that can connect horizontally. These hydra-like entities periodically emerge across space and time. They thrive through a rich web of connections that grow below the visible surface. And in our interconnected world, this is where we can focus our efforts. Complexity practitioners have pointed to fungus threads called mycelia that connect living plants underground sharing nutrients and information. Paul Stamets, fungi expert, calls them the Earth's natural internet.[15] The lesson for us is how to animate and extend this information superhighway between geographically disparate projects to super-charge unlocking sustainable urban futures.

Connections and capacities that flow through these networks can be built up through peer-to-peer and collaborative networks. We already have templates for this in the World Social Forums and the Occupy movement, workers, housing and platform cooperatives as well as digital tools such as Creative Commons Licensing, Skills Commons and the Wiki Foundation. Seen as such, the task is not just about scaling up particular place-based activity, although of course this is crucial. We also need to foster the conditions for this networked micropolitics to spread mimetically and virally. Moments of critical mass can be reached that can infiltrate and corrode dominant ways of organising. And rather than just focusing on growth in absolute numbers, we need to be alive to qualitative development especially the quality of interpersonal relations and issues of caring, nurturing and solidarity. The impact of particular projects can be underestimated when they are assessed in terms of their visible, numerical and institutional impact.

* * *

Whether you are a policy maker, politician, researcher, entrepreneur or activist, there are actions that can be done right now to unlock real change. As I have stressed, this will involve imagination, exper-imentation, compassion and also a degree of risk and courage. It will require making new and sometimes difficult connections, as well as a commitment to transformation. While this is the end of the book, I hope it also marks the beginning of new opportunities, or for those already on a journey supports ongoing social change work. To this end, I have set up a website at www.unlockingsustainablecities.org, where people can connect and share ideas and initiatives. Commit to acting now and start small. But remember, if we are to unlock real change, think big.

A Brief Manifesto for Real Change

By way of concluding this journey through Unlocking Sustainable Cities I bring together some of the key ideas through a brief manifesto. These are not intended to be an exhaustive or detailed guide for how it will all work out in practice. Instead, I summarise some principles and directions that underpin actions that anyone, including citizens, policy makers, practitioners, innovators, researchers and social activists, can explore and discuss. While they are broad and ambitious, they are also realistic, doable and ultimately necessary if we want to unlock real urban change. They are an intervention and invitation to explore what future urban sustainability could be like. Ultimately, they will mean different things in different places, and I would love to have a continued dialogue with readers on this through the book's website.

The Car-Free City

1. The first pillar of this manifesto, car-free cities, requires committing to significantly moving away from private motorised vehicles and dedicating less space to them.
2. To ensure a smooth transition, workable, extensive and affordable alternatives have to be powered up before a broad power down of car infrastructure occurs.
3. The immediate mass roll out of small steps towards car-free cities will be crucial: city-wide very low emission zones, prioritising road safety, shifts to zero-emission vehicles and car-lite urban design that prioritise walking, cycling and the many forms of zero-emission rapid transit such as trolley buses, trams, light rail, subways and street cars.
4. Brave decisions to reallocate infrastructure dedicated to private vehicles including highways, car parks and retail malls are urgently required on a mass scale.
5. Lock into future options around driverless cars need to be avoided, as they do not shift cities away from car culture.
6. Radical re-zoning will need to be undertaken through a reorientation of the planning system as well as primary legislation, and a

new approach to weaving together work, food, leisure and home environments in ways that directly eliminate the need for cars.

7. Subsidies and research grants locked up in supporting fossil fuel based private vehicles need to be rapidly withdrawn and redirected at unlocking car-free urban mobility options.

8. Coalitions of citizens and innovators need to take the lead and push the agenda to show what is possible to reduce car dependency through changes in daily mobility practices.

9. Municipalities will still play a central role especially in terms of starting city-owned transit systems that can avoid locking into high value, socially uneven corporate-led options.

10. There needs to be a focus on the wider issue of urban mobility, connectivity and sharing between multiple mobility options rather than backing single likely future winners.

11. Creating socially just patterns of urban mobility is essential, especially in terms of locking down historic patterns of transport injustices and creating very broad participation in the design of mobility systems.

12. Shifts in advertising and marketing are required to create new values and social stimuli that downplay car culture and celebrate sustainable mobility.

13. Given the increasingly deadly consequences of locking into urban car use, citizen organising of, for example, car-free events, billboard subvertising or impromptu road closures will be crucial in highlighting priorities for change.

The Post-Carbon City

1. The second pillar, the post-carbon city, requires holistic and interconnected action and ideas across a broad range of areas: infrastructure, work, governance, culture, education, leisure, mobility, health.

2. Municipalities will play a key role in setting ambitious net zero-carbon and renewable energy plans, and they will require significant new powers to prohibit polluting and climate unsafe activities.

3. City-owned entities need to lead the way in creating and distributing affordable, locally generated green energy.

4. All new neighbourhood planning needs reorienting around zero-carbon living arrangements, designing out energy use and designing in low-impact travel, work and leisure options.

5. Primary legislation will be required to break up the brown fuel sector.

6. A huge subsidy transfer is required away from centralised and corporate energy providers to a constellation of civic energy ones.

7. Difficult choices need to be pursued to curtail and reduce energy demand, especially around hyper-consumerism and poor city zoning.

8. The potential of civic energy and local smart grids needs unleashing through regulatory changes and stimulating innovation so that every building becomes a power station.

9. Citizen groups are best placed to design, implement and manage local energy systems. Their power needs unleashing through enabling finance and regulations so they can lead the civic energy revolution.

10. Given the scale of the task and the sluggishness of the response in the face of mounting climate breakdown, coalitions of groups taking direct action will play a role in the lock down of unsustainable and dangerous activities.

The Bio City

1. The third pillar, the bio city, rests on recognising and nurturing more co-dependent relationships between humans, non human species and natural systems.

2. This is a generational task and will in particular require a fundamental redesign of how we approach education.

3. Restoring and regenerating urban nature needs to become central drivers of all urban development decisions, especially in the context of promoting climate-safe and resilient cities.

4. Biophilic and biomimetic design are key to help us reconnect with, learn from and emulate natural processes in cities in ways that can underpin human flourishing.

5. Natural features ranging from linear parks and vertical green walls to rain gardens and breathing buildings offer a whole basket of benefits and need to be built in and retrofitted to all urban developments.

6. Due to their proximity and daily experiences, local residents are best placed to steward and regenerate nature in their communities.

7. Connecting and enhancing blue and green urban infrastructures can unlock the significant potential of urban nature, and embed water-sensitive design that can tackle extreme weather changes.
8. All options and potentials for food growing within urban spaces need to be unlocked, especially in ways that foster significant changes in urban forms and functions.
9. Given the rapid annihilation of animal species globally, spaces for urban wildlife require urgently protecting and enhancing.

The Common City

1. The fourth pillar, the common city, requires shifting as many urban resources and assets as possible into common ownership.
2. Municipalities need to recover full control over city planning, and implement a pro-citizen, socially just approach to all urban development.
3. Mechanisms are required to facilitate broad and meaningful citizen input into, scrutiny over, and management of, major city decisions especially around the allocation of resources and land.
4. Vacant and derelict land, especially in corporate land banks, needs reallocating to community-owned organisations.
5. Shifts in taxation from income to land are required to break up historically high levels of unequal land ownership.
6. The role of the local state becomes enabler and facilitator of community- and citizen-led initiatives that can unlock inclusion, ecological restoration and local wealth creation.
7. Commonly owned institutions, worker-owned cooperatives and complementary money systems are required to capture and recirculate value and build community wealth.
8. The mass release and use of data is required to empower communities to engage with, and steer, local development.
9. New measures and metrics based on happiness, well-being and sustainability are required that can shift priorities away from business-as-usual economic growth.
10. Learning and research programmes and paid work release will facilitate broad engagement with civic democracy.
11. Citizen movements that undertake civil disobedience and direct action will play a vital role in highlighting the shortcomings of established legal and democratic processes and priority areas for action.

Cross-Cutting Issues

1. Direct national and international legislation is required to enhance and empower city-based actions.

2. City authorities can play an enabling role at the centre of these changes, working alongside citizen groups, private entrepreneurs and academic researchers.

3. Cities have to start from where they are and what they have. From tower blocks and car parks to highways and green spaces, repurposing and retrofitting what already exists will be a crucial aspect of the future sustainable city.

4. Rethinking both the form and function of city systems will be the key to unlocking real potential. This will involve slow, difficult and unpopular decisions in the short-term especially around re-zoning and the reallocation of resources and activities.

5. Socially just methods and outcomes and a broad commitment to participation need to be central to whatever changes occur.

6. Techniques including community organising, co-production, learning by doing, action research, restorative practices and facilitation support will be central to build broad support and minimise conflict.

7. The hardest point to accept is that all of us, in countless and complex ways (large and small, visible and invisible), are responsible for creating our deeply unsustainable world. But more positively, we can all be part of the great unlocking of sustainable urban futures.

Notes

ACKNOWLEDGEMENTS

1. J. McKay and B. Dickson, *Dreams of a Low Carbon Future* (Leeds: University of Leeds, 2013).

INTRODUCTION

1. Excellent online resources exist which document this wealth of radical urban innovation projects, such as the New Europe website (available at: www.citiesintransition.eu, accessed 31 January 2018).
2. For a sample of good introductory texts to critical issues facing cities, see H. Girardet, *Creating Regenerative Cities* (Abingdon: Routledge, 2015); D. Harvey, *Rebel Cities: From the Right to the City to the Urban Revolution* (London: Verso, 2012); N. Brenner, P. Marcuse and M. Mayer (eds), *Cities for People, Not for Profit: Critical Urban Theory and the Right to the City* (Abingdon: Routledge, 2012); A. Minton, *Ground Control: Fear and Happiness in the Twenty-First-Century City* (London: Penguin, 2009); S. Zukin, *Naked City: The Death and Life of Authentic Urban Places* (Oxford: Oxford University Press, 2010); and A. Merrifield, *The New Urban Question* (London: Pluto Press, 2014).
3. R. Tyszczuk, *Provisional Cities Cautionary Tales for the Anthropocene* (London: Routledge, 2018).
4. Y. Parag and K. Janda, 'More than Filler: Middle Actors and Socio-Technical Change in the Energy System from the "Middle-Out"', *Energy Research and Social Science* 3 (2014): 102–112; and S. Eizaguirre, M. Pradel, A. Terrones, X. Martinez-Celorrio and M. García, 'Multilevel Governance and Social Cohesion: Bringing Back Conflict in Citizenship Practices', *Urban Studies* 49 (2012): 1999–2016.
5. J. Holloway and A. Grubačić, *In, Against, and Beyond Capitalism: The San Francisco Lectures* (Oakland, CA: PM Press, 2016).

6. M. DeLanda, *A New Philosophy of Society: Assemblage Theory and Social Complexity* (London: Continuum, 2006).

7. Here I am inspired by the work of Paul Gilbert, see P. Gilbert, *The Compassionate Mind* (London: Constable & Robinson, 2013).

8. Cittaslow: International Network of Cities Where Living is Good website (available at: www.cittaslow.org, accessed 8 February 2018). See also H. Mayer and P. Knox, 'Slow Cities: Sustainable Places in a Fast World', *Journal of Urban Affairs* 28/4 (2006): 321–334.

9. G. Roelvink, K. St Martin and J.K. Gibson-Graham (eds), *Making Other Worlds Possible: Performing Diverse Economies* (Minneapolis, MN: University of Minnesota Press, 2015).

10. R. Solnit, *Hope in the Dark: Untold Histories, Wild Possibilities* (New York: Nation Books, 2006).

11. Ibid.

12. S. Gerhardt, *Why Love Matters: How Affection Shapes a Baby's Brain* (New York: Brunner-Routledge, 2004).

13. Q. Stevens, *The Ludic City: Exploring the Potential of Public Spaces* (Abingdon: Routledge, 2007).

14. J. Evans, A. Karvonen and R. Raven (eds), *The Experimental City* (Abingdon: Routledge, 2016).

15. E. Cahn, *No More Throw-Away People: The Co-Production Imperative* (Washington, DC: Essential Books, 2004).

16. D. Meadows, D. Meadows, J. Randers and W. Behrens, *Limits to Growth: A Report for the Club of Rome's Project on the Predicament of Mankind* (New York: Universe Books, 1972); and E.F. Schumacher, *Small is Beautiful: A Study of Economics as if People Mattered* (London: Blond & Briggs, 1973).

17. See J. Mander and E. Goldsmith (eds), *The Case Against the Global Economy and for a Turn Towards the Local* (Berkeley, CA: University of California Press, 2002); U. Rossi, *Cities in Global Capitalism* (Cambridge: Polity Press, 2017); and N. Brenner and N. Theodore (eds), *Spaces of Neoliberalism: Urban Restructuring in North America and Western Europe* (Malden: Blackwell Publishing, 2002).

1.   THE CAR-FREE CITY

1. P. Wollen and J. Kerr (eds), *Autopia: Cars and Culture* (London: Reaktion Books, 2002); D. Miller (ed), *Car Cultures* (Oxford: Berg,

2001); and J. Conley and A.T. McLaren (eds), *Car Troubles: Critical Studies of Automobility and Auto-Mobility* (Abingdon: Routledge, 2009).

2. See J. Crawford, Carfree Cities website (2016) (available at: www.carfree.com/intro_cfc.html, accessed 9 February 2018).

3. US Census, 'Motor Vehicle Registration 2000' (available at: www.allcountries.org/uscensus/1027_motor_vehicle_registrations.html, accessed 9 February 2018).

4. J. Voelcker, '1.2 Billion Vehicles On World's Roads Now, 2 Billion By 2035: Report', 2014 (available at: www.greencarreports.com/news/1093560_1-2-billion-vehicles-on-worlds-roads-now-2-billion-by-2035-report, accessed 9 February 2018).

5. Report. 'Organization of Motor Vehicle Manufacturers Global Production Figures' (available at: http://www.oica.net/production-statistics/, accessed 9 February 2018).

6. Department for Transport, 'Road Traffic Forecasts 2015' (available at: www.gov.uk/government/uploads/system/uploads/attachment_data/file/411471/road-traffic-forecasts-2015.pdf, accessed 9 February 2018).

7. J.B. DeLong, *Slouching Towards Utopia: The Economic History of the Twentieth Century* (London: Profile Books, 2016).

8. K. Sheth, 'Top Motor Vehicle Producing Countries', 2017 (available at: www.worldatlas.com/articles/top-motor-vehicle-producing-countries.html, accessed 9 February 2018).

9. OICA, 'The World's Automotive Industry: Some Key Figures', 2006 (available at: oica.net/wp-content/uploads/2007/06/oica-depliant-final.pdf, accessed 9 February 2018).

10. B. Tuttle, 'What Happens When We Reach "Peak Car"?', *Time*, 25 September 2012 (available at: http://business.time.com/2012/09/25/what-happens-when-we-reach-peak-car/, accessed 9 February 2018).

11. 'Fortune 500' (available at: fortune.com/fortune500/, accessed 9 February 2018).

12. European Environment Agency, 'Investment in Transport Infrastructure', 2016 (available at: www.eea.europa.eu/publications/technical_report_2007_3, accessed 9 February 2018).

13. Eurostat, 'Oil and Petroleum Products – A Statistical Overview', 2017 (available at: ec.europa.eu/eurostat/statistics-explained/

index.php/Oil_and_petroleum_products_-_a_statistical_overview, accessed 9 February 2018).

14. U.S. Energy Information Administration, 'U.S. Energy Facts Explained', 2017 (available at: www.eia.gov/energyexplained/index. cfm?page=us_energy_home, accessed 9 February 2018).

15. OPEC means the Organization of the Petroleum Exporting Countries an intergovernmental organisation of 14 nations accounting for nearly half of global oil production and three quarters of the world's proven oil reserves.

16. S. Goddard, *Getting There: The Epic Struggle Between Road and Rail in the American Century* (Chicago, IL: University of Chicago Press, 1996).

17. For an account of the USA, see J. Kay, *Asphalt Nation: How the Automobile Took Over America and How We Can Take It Back* (New York: Crown Publishing, 1997). For the UK, see C. Pooley, *Mobility, Migration and Transport: Historical Perspectives* (London: Palgrave Macmillan, 2017).

18. C. Gardner, 'We Are the 25%: Looking at Street Area Percentages and Surface Parking', 2011 (available at: oldurbanist.blogspot. co.uk/2011/12/we-are-25-looking-at-street-area.html, accessed 9 February 2018).

19. S. Frizell, 'L.A. Drivers Spend 90 Hours a Year Stuck in Traffic, Study Finds', *Time*, 4 June 2014 (available at: www.time.com/2821738/los-angeles-traffic-study, accessed 13 February 2018).

20. 'Motorists Spend 106 Days Looking for Parking Spots', *The Telegraph*, 27 May 2013 (available at: www.telegraph.co.uk/ motoring/news/10082461/Motorists-spend-106-days-looking-for-parking-spots.html, accessed 13 February 2018).

21. World Carfree Network, 'Global Charter', 2012, (available at: www.worldcarfree.net/about_us/global/charter.php, accessed 13 February 2018).

22. World Health Organization, 'Ambient (Outdoor) Air Quality and Health – Fact Sheet', (2016) (available at: www.who.int/mediacentre/ factsheets/fs313/en/, accessed 13 February 2018).

23. Royal College of Physicians, 'Every Breath We Take: The Lifelong Impact of Air Pollution', report of a working party (London: Royal College of Physicians, 2016).

24. R. Rohde and R. Muller, 'Air Pollution in China: Mapping of Concentrations and Sources', *PLoS ONE* 10/8 (2015): e0135749.

25. World Health Organization, 'WHO Air Quality Guidelines for Particulate Matter, Ozone, Nitrogen Dioxide and Sulfur Dioxide: Global Update 2005' (available at: apps.who.int/iris/bitstream/10665/69477/1/WHO_SDE_PHE_OEH_06.02_eng.pdf, accessed 13 February 2018).

26. World Health Organization, 'WHO Global Urban Ambient Air Pollution Database', (2016) (available at: www.who.int/phe/health_topics/outdoorair/databases/cities/en/, accessed 13 February 2018).

27. Royal College of Physicians, 'Lancet Countdown 2017 Report: Briefing for UK Policymakers' (available at: www.rcplondon.ac.uk/news/research-shows-44-uk-cities-breach-world-health-organization-guidelines-air-pollution, accessed 13 February 2018).

28. L. Mangaldas, 'Delhi's Government Declares a Public Health Emergency as Air Pollution Chokes the City', *Forbes*, 8 November 2017 (available at: www.forbes.com/sites/leezamangaldas/2017/11/08/delhis-government-declares-a-public-health-emergency-as-air-pollution-chokes-the-city/#3256107b2a5a, accessed 13 February 2018).

29. R. Russell-Jones, 'Dirty Diesel', *British Medical Journal* 365 (2016): i6726 (available at: www.bmj.com/content/355/bmj.i6726, accessed 13 February 2018).

30. M. Le Page, 'UK Loses Another Court Case over Failure to Tackle Air Pollution', *New Scientist*, 27 April 2017 (available at: www.newscientist.com/article/2129210-uk-loses-another-court-case-over-failure-to-tackle-air-pollution/, accessed 13 February 2018).

31. I. Torjesen, 'NICE Issues Guidance on Policies to Reduce Vehicle Emissions', *British Medical Journal* 355 (2016): i6453 (available at: www.bmj.com/content/355/bmj.i6453.full, accessed 13 February 2018); and 'The UK Health Alliance on Climate Change's Response to Defra's Open Consultation on the Implementation of Clean Air Zones in England' (available at: www.bma.org.uk/-/media/files/pdfs/collective%20voice/policy%20research/public%20and%20population%20health/uk-health-alliance-draft-response-defra-consultation-clean-air-zones.pdf?la=en, accessed 13 February 2018).

32. B. Plumer, 'The Rapid Growth of Electric Cars Worldwide, in 4 Charts', *Vox*, 6 June 2016 (available at: www.vox.com/2016/6/6/11867894/electric-cars-global-sales, accessed 20 February 2018).

33. World Health Organization, 'Road Traffic Injuries: Fact Sheet', 2018 (available at: www.who.int/mediacentre/factsheets/fs358/en/, accessed 20 February 2018).

34. Ibid.

35. See Goal 3.6 in: United Nations, 'Transforming Our World: the 2030 Agenda for Sustainable Development', 2015 (available at: sustainabledevelopment.un.org/post2015/transformingourworld, accessed 20 February 2018).

36. Public Health England, 'Health Matters: Obesity and the Food Environment', 2017 (available at: www.gov.uk/government/publications/health-matters-obesity-and-the-food-environment/health-matters-obesity-and-the-food-environment--2, accessed 20 February 2018).

37. K. Lucas, 'Transport and Social Exclusion: Where are We Now?', *Transport Policy* 20 (2012): 105–113; C. Mullen and G. Marsden, 'Mobility Justice in Low Carbon Energy Transitions', *Energy Research & Social Science* 18 (2016): 109–117; and K. Martens, *Transport Justice: Designing Fair Transportation Systems* (New York: Routledge, 2016).

38. T. Stacey and L. Shaddock, 'Taken for a Ride – How UK Public Transport Subsidies Entrench Inequality' (London: The Equality Trust, 2015) (available at: www.equalitytrust.org.uk/taken-ride-how-uk-public-transport-subsidies-entrench-inequality, accessed 20 February 2018).

39. S. Raphael, A. Berube and E. Deakin, 'Socioeconomic Differences in Household Automobile Ownership Rates: Implications for Evaluation Policy', 2006, University of California Transport Centre Earlier Faculty Research Series, no. 804 (available at: escholarship.org/uc/item/7bp4n2f6, accessed 20 February 2018).

40. C. Lane, 'Rapid Transit is Key to Building Equitable Cities', (2016), Next City website op-ed (available at: nextcity.org/daily/entry/new-urban-agenda-transit, accessed 20 February 2018).

41. R. Diekstra and M. Kroon, 'Cars and Behaviour: Psychological Barriers to Car Restraint and Sustainable Urban Transport', *Sustainable Transport* (2003): 252–264; L. Steg, 'Car Use: Lust and Must. Instrumental, Symbolic and Affective Motives for Car Use', *Transportation Research Part A: Policy and Practice* 39/2–3 (2005): 147–162.

42. 'The Billionaires Club: Only 36 Companies Have $1,000 Million-PlusAdBudgets'(availableat:www.businessinsider.com/the-35-companies-that-spent-1-billion-on-ads-in-2011-2012-11?IR=T, accessed 20 February 2018).

43. T. Sager and S. Bergmann, *The Ethics of Mobilities: Rethinking Place, Exclusion, Freedom and Environment* (London: Routledge, 2008).

44. N. Foletta and J. Henderson, *Low Car(bon) Communities: Inspiring Car-Free and Car-Lite Urban Futures* (Abingdon: Routledge, 2016); and J.H. Crawford, *Carfree Cities* (Utrecht: International Books, 2000).

45. 'Cars Traditionally Unwelcome on Nantucket Island', 2007, MotorCities National Heritage Area website (available at: www.motorcities.org/Story/+Cars+Traditionally+Unwelcome+on+Nantucket+Island-25.html, accessed 20 February 2018).

46. G. McKay (ed.), *DiY Culture: Party & Protest in Nineties Britain* (London: Verso, 1998).

47. J. Jordan, 'Case Study: Reclaim the Streets', Beautiful Trouble website (available at: beautifultrouble.org/case/reclaim-the-streets/, accessed 20 February 2018).

48. T. Mertes (ed.), *A Movement of Movements: Is Another World Really Possible?* (London: Verso, 2003).

49. World Carfree Network website (available at: www.worldcarfree. net, accessed 20 February 2018).

50. 'Mapa Ciclovía [Cycle Path Map]', Bogotá District Institute for Recreation and Sports (available at: www.idrd.gov.co/sitio/idrd/content/mapa-ciclovia, accessed 21 February 2018).

51. M. Ariff, 'Jakarta's Car-Free Day', *New Straits Times*, 17 January 2017 (available at: www.nst.com.my/news/2017/01/205016/jakartas-car-free-day, accessed 21 February 2018).

52. See Raahgiri Days website (available at: www.raahgiridays.com, accessed 21 February 2018).

53. R. Aldred, 'The New Mobilities Paradigm and Sustainable Transport: Finding Synergies and Creating New Methods', in S. Lockie, D. Sonnenfeld and D. Fisher (eds), *Routledge International Handbook of Social and Environmental Change* (Abingdon: Routledge, 2014), 190–204.

54. A. Cathart-Keays, 'Two-Wheel Takeover: Bikes Outnumber Cars for the First Time in Copenhagen', *The Guardian*, 30 November 2016 (available at: www.theguardian.com/cities/2016/nov/30/

cycling-revolution-bikes-outnumber-cars-first-time-copenhagen-denmark, accessed 21 February 2018).

55. Ibid.

56. J. Sadik-Khan and S. Solomonow, *Streetfight: Handbook for an Urban Revolution* (New York: Viking, 2016).

57. J. Gehl, *Life Between Buildings: Using Public Space* (New York: Van Nostrand Reinhold, 1987).

58. A. Walker, 'Six Freeway Removals that Changed Their Cities Forever', Gizmodo website, 25 May 2016 (available at: gizmodo.com/6-freeway-removals-that-changed-their-cities-forever-1548314937, accessed 21 February 2018).

59. Wikipedia, 'List of Car-Free Spaces' (available at: en.wikipedia.org/wiki/List_of_car-free_places, accessed 21 February 2018).

60. See Park(ing) Day DIY Planning Network website (available at: my.parkingday.org/, accessed 23 February 2018).

61. See Playing Out website (available at: playingout.net, accessed 23 February).

62. L. Bliss, 'Oslo is On Track for a Car-Free Future', *Citylab*, 13 April 2017 (available at: www.citylab.com/transportation/2017/04/oslo-is-on-track-for-a-car-free-future/522882/, accessed 23 February 2018).

63. C. Celis-Morales, D. Lyall, P. Welsh *et al.*, 'Association between Active Commuting and Incident Cardiovascular Disease, Cancer, and Mortality: Prospective Cohort Study', *British Medical Journal* (2017): 357:j1456.

64. See MaaS (Mobility as a Service) Alliance website (available at: maas-alliance.eu, accessed 23 February 2018).

65. World Resources Institute, 'TransCarioca Bus Rapid Transit (BRT) Arrives in Rio de Janeiro, Brazil', 2014 (available at: www.wrirosscities.org/news/transcarioca-bus-rapid-transit-brt-arrives-rio-de-janeiro-brazil, accessed 23 February 2018).

66. J. Whitelegg, *Mobility: A New Urban Design and Transport Planning Philosophy for a Sustainable Future* (CreateSpace Independent Publishing Platform, 2016).

2.   THE POST-CARBON CITY

1. There are many insightful books that explore energy use in cities. See, for example, A. Troy, *The Very Hungry City: Urban Energy Efficiency*

and the Economic Fate of Cities (New Haven, CT: Yale University Press, 2014); and H. Margalit, *Energy, Cities and Sustainability: An Historical Approach* (Abingdon: Routledge, 2016).

2. R. Heinberg, *The Party's Over: Oil War and the Fate of Industrial Societies* (Gabriola Island, BC: New Society Publishers, 2005).

3. UN Habitat, 'Energy', 2012 (available at: unhabitat.org/urban-themes/energy/, accessed 23 February 2018).

4. C. Brahic, 'Humanity's Carbon Budget Set at One Trillion Tonnes', *New Scientist*, 29 April 2009 (available at: www.newscientist.com/article/dn17051-humanitys-carbon-budget-set-at-one-trillion-tonnes/, accessed 23 February 2018).

5. 350.org, 'Climate Science Basics' (available at: 350.org/science/, accessed 23 February 2018).

6. See Beyond Zero Emissions website (available at: bze.org.au, accessed 23 February 2018).

7. European Commission, '2050 Low-Carbon Economy', 2018 (available at: ec.europa.eu/clima/policies/strategies/2050_en, accessed 23 February 2018).

8. R. Lowes, 'Who owns the UK's Energy Distribution Networks?', 2017, Exeter Energy Policy Group blog (available at: blogs.exeter.ac.uk/energy/2017/05/25/who-owns-the-uks-energy-distribution-networks/, accessed 23 February 2018).

9. US Energy Information Administration, 'What is U.S. Electricity Generation by Energy Source?', 2017 (available at: www.eia.gov/tools/faqs/faq.php?id=427&t=3, accessed 23 February 2018).

10. UK Department for Business, Energy & Industrial Strategy, 'Statistical Press Release: UK Energy Statistics, 2016 & Q4 2016', 2017 (available at: www.gov.uk/government/uploads/system/uploads/attachment_data/file/604695/Press_Notice_March_2017.pdf, accessed 23 February 2018).

11. F. Creutzig, G. Baiocchi, R. Bierkandt, P. Pichler and K. Seto, 'Global Typology of Urban Energy Use and Potentials for an Urbanization Mitigation Wedge', *PNAS* 112/20 (2015): 6283–6288.

12. F. Schmidt-Bleek, 'Factor 10: The Future of Stuff', *Sustainability: Science, Practice & Policy* 4/1 (2008) (available at: web.archive.org/web/20120426072144/http://sspp.proquest.com/archives/vol4iss1/editorial.schmidt-bleek.html, accessed 23 February 2018).

13. A. Howard, '"Delivering on 2 Degrees": Kevin Anderson Presents "Triumph and Tragedy in Paris" at the University of Sheffield, 28th

April 2016', Carbon Neutral University Network blog (available at: www.carbonneutraluniversity.org/delivering-on-2-degrees---kevin-anderson.html, accessed 23 February 2018).

14. G. D'Alisa, F. Demaria and G. Kallis (eds), *Degrowth: A Vocabulary for a New Era* (Abingdon: Routledge, 2014).

15. See Post Carbon Institute website (available at: www.postcarbon.org, accessed 23 February 2018).

16. D. Lerch, 'Post Carbon Cities: Planning for Energy and Climate Uncertainty', guidebook, Post Carbon Institute, 2007 (available at: www.postcarbon.org/publications/post-carbon-cities/, accessed 23 February 2018).

17. R. Heinberg and D. Lerch (eds), *The Post Carbon Reader: Managing the 21st Century's Sustainability Crises* (Healdsburg, CA: Watershed Media, 2010).

18. D. Hoornweg, M. Freire, M. Lee, P. Bhada-Tata and B. Yuen, 'Cities and Climate Change: Responding to an Urgent Agenda', report, The World Bank Urban Development Series, Washington, DC, 2011 (available at: http://documents.worldbank.org/curated/en/613201468149671438/Main-report, accessed 23 February 2018).

19. Global Footprint Network, 'Ecological Footprint' (available at: www.footprintnetwork.org/our-work/ecological-footprint/, accessed 23 February 2018).

20. P. Desai and P. King, *One Planet Living: A Guide To Enjoying Life On Our One Planet* (London: Alaistair Sawday, 2006).

21. See Contraction & Convergence (C&C) Climate Truth & Reconciliation website (available at: www.gci.org.uk, accessed 23 February 2018).

22. R. Heinberg, *Power Down: Options and Actions for Post-Carbon World* (Gabriola Island, BC: New Society Publishers, 2004).

23. M. Kemp (ed.), 'Zero Carbon Britain 2030: A New Energy Strategy', report, Zero Carbon Britain research project, Centre for Alternative Technology, 2010 (available at: www.zerocarbonbritain.org/en/zcb-publications, accessed 23 February 2018).

24. A. Fenderson, 'Energy Descent Action Plans – A Primer', *Resilience*, 7 June 2006 (available at: www.resilience.org/stories/2006-06-07/energy-descent-action-plans-primer-0/, accessed 23 February 2018).

25. D. Holmgren, *Future Scenarios: How Communities Can Adapt to Peak Oil and Climate Change* (White River Junction, VT: Chelsea Green, 2009).

26. Ecological Sequestration Trust, 'Approach' (available at: ecoseques trust.org/about-us/our-approach/, accessed 23 February 2018).

27. J. Rifkin, *The Third Industrial Revolution: How Lateral Power is Transforming Energy, the Economy, and the World* (New York: St Martin's Press, 2011).

28. Climate Smart Cities, 'Leeds City Region', 2012 (available at: www.climatesmartcities.org/case-studies, accessed 23 February 2018).

29. C40 Cities Climate Leadership Group and Arup, 'Working Together: Global Aggregation of City Climate Agreements', 2014 (available at: www.arup.com/projects/global-aggregation-of-city-climate-commitments-report, accessed 23 February 2018).

30. United Nations Environment Programme, 'The Emissions Gap Report 2014' (available at: web.unep.org/emissionsgap/resources, accessed 23 February 2018).

31. C40 Cities and Arup, 'Deadline 2020: How Cities will get the Job Done' (available at: www.c40.org/other/deadline_2020, accessed 23 February 2018).

32. Global Covenant of Mayors for Climate & Energy, 'Global Covenant Cities', interactive map (available at: www.globalcovenantofmayors.org/cities/, accessed 23 February 2018).

33. CDMX (Ciudad de Mexico), SEDEMA (Secretaría del Medico Ambiente) and C40 Cities, 'Mexico City's Climate Action Program 2014-2020: Progress Report 2016' (available at: www.data.sedema.cdmx.gob.mx/cambioclimaticocdmx/images/biblioteca_cc/PACCM-ingles.pdf, accessed 23 February 2018).

34. City of Vancouver, 'Renewable City Strategy: Our future to 2050', 2018 (available at: vancouver.ca/green-vancouver/renewable-city.aspx, accessed 23 February 2018).

35. World Business Council for Sustainable Development, 'Zero Emissions Cities' (available at: www.wbcsd.org/Projects/Zero-Emissions-Cities, accessed 23 February 2018).

36. New York State, 'Reforming the Energy Vision (REV): Building a Clean, More Resilient, and Affordable Energy System for all New Yorkers' (available at: rev.ny.gov, accessed 23 February 2018).

37. Bioregional, 'BedZED' (available at: www.bioregional.com/bedzed/, accessed 23 February 2018).

38. P. Chatterton, 'Towards an Agenda for Post-Carbon Cities: Lessons from Lilac, the UK's First Ecological, Affordable Cohousing Community', *International Journal of Urban and Regional Research* 37/5 (2013): 1654–1674.

39. S. Hall, T. Foxon and R. Bolton, 'The New "Civic" Energy Sector: Civil Society Institutions and Energy Infrastructure Transitions in Germany and the UK', working paper, Realising Transition Pathways, 2015 (available at: www.realisingtransitionpathways. org.uk/realisingtransitionpathways/publications/Working_papers_ and_reports/RTP_Working_Paper_2015_01.pdf, accessed 23 February 2018).

40. A. Moodie, 'These 5 U.S. Towns are Powered Entirely by Renewable Energy', *HuffPost*, 1 November 2017 (available at: www.huffington post.com/entry/american-cities-powered-by-renewable-energy_ us_59ea2cbee4b0958c4681d32a, accessed 23 February 2018).

41. J. Schlandt, 'Small, but Powerful – Germany's Municipal Utilities', *Clean Energy Wire*, 18 February 2015 (available at: www.clean energywire.org/factsheets/small-powerful-germanys-municipal- utilities, accessed 23 February 2018).

42. Stadtwerke München (Munich Municipal Utilities), 'SWM Renewable Energies Expansion Campaign' (available at: www.swm. de/english/company/energy-generation/renewable-energies.html, accessed 23 February 2018).

43. Green City Energy, 'Our Objective: To Combine Economy with Ecology' (available at: www.greencity-energy.com/about-us/, accessed 23 February 2018).

44. A. Leidreiter, 'Renewables Rising – Community Energy Rising', World Future Council: The Blog of the Climate & Energy Commission, 2016 (available at: www.power-to-the-people.net/ 2016/06/renewables-rising-community-energy-rising/, accessed 23 February 2018).

45. L. Laybourn-Langton, 'Community and Local Energy: Challenges and Opportunities', report, Institute for Public Policy Research, 2016 (available at: www.ippr.org/files/publications/pdf/community- energy_June2016.pdf, accessed 23 February 2017).

46. See Powerhouse website (available at: www.powerhouse.solar, accessed 23 February 2018).

47. See Repowering London website (available at: www.repowering. org.uk, accessed 23 February 2018).

48. S. Faris, 'The Solar Company Making a Profit on Poor Africans', *Bloomberg*, 2 December 2015 (available at: www.bloomberg.com/features/2015-mkopa-solar-in-africa/, accessed 23 February 2018).

49. T. Swagerty, 'Pollinate Energy (Bangalore, India)', Permaculature Research Institute, 2013 (available at: www.permaculturenews.org/2013/09/04/pollinate-energy-bangalore-india/, 23 February 2018).

50. N. Klein, *This Changes Everything: Capitalism vs. The Climate* (New York: Simon & Schuster, 2014).

51. Climate Justice Now!, 'Call for "System Change not Climate Change" Unites Global Movement', 2010 (available at: www.viacampesina.org/en/call-for-system-change-not-climate-change-unites-global-movement/, accessed 23 February 2018).

52. See FracTracker Alliance website (available at: www.fractracker.org, accessed 23 February 2018).

3. THE BIO CITY

1. D. Haraway, *Simians, Cyborgs and Women: The Reinvention of Nature* (New York: Routledge, 1991).

2. M. Bookchin, *The Ecology of Freedom: The Emergence and Dissolution of Hierarchy* (Palo Alto, CA: Chesire Books, 1982).

3. R. Wokler and N. Geras, *Enlightenment and Modernity* (London: Palgrave, 2000).

4. P. Linebaugh, *Stop, Thief!: The Commons, Enclosures, and Resistance* (Oakland, CA: PM Press, 2014).

5. M. Perelman, *The Invention of Capitalism: Classical Political Economy and the Secret History of Primitive Accumulation* (Durham, NC: Duke University Press, 2000).

6. E. Griffin, *A Short History of the British Industrial Revolution* (New York: Palgrave Macmillan, 2010).

7. B. Norman, *Sustainable Pathways for our Cities and Regions: Planning within Planetary Boundaries* (Abingdon: Routledge, 2018).

8. N. Brenner (ed.), *Implosions/Explosions: Towards a Study of Planetary Urbanization* (Berlin: Jovis, 2014).

9. D. Haraway, *Staying with the Trouble: Making Kin in the Chthulucene* (Durham, NC: Duke University Press, 2016).

10. D. McGregor, D. Simon and D. Thompson (eds), *The Peri-Urban Interface: Approaches to Sustainable Natural and Human Resource Use* (London: Earthscan, 2006).

11. Rockefeller Foundation, 'Decision Intelligence Document: Degradation and Loss of Peri-Urban Ecosystems', 2013 (available at: assets.rockefellerfoundation.org/app/uploads/20130528221316/ Degredation-and-Loss-of-Peri-Urban-Systems.pdf, accessed 26 February 2018).

12. N. Castree, *Nature* (Abingdon: Routledge, 2005).

13. D.W. Hall (ed.), *Victorian Ecocriticism: The Politics of Place and Early Environmental Justice* (Lanham, MD: Rowman & Littlefield, 2017).

14. R. Watson, *Back to Nature: The Green and the Real in the Late Renaissance* (Philadelphia, PA: University of Pennsylvania Press, 2006).

15. R. Carson, *Silent Spring* (Boston, MA: Houghton Mifflin, 1962).

16. D. Meadows, D. Meadows, J. Randers and W. Behrens, *Limits to Growth: A Report for the Club of Rome's Project on the Predicament of Mankind* (New York: Universe Books, 1972).

17. G. Brundtland, M. Khalid, S. Agnelli, *et al.*, 'Our Common Future ("The Brundtland Report")', report for the Brundtland Commission (Oxford: Oxford University, 1987).

18. United Nations, 'Goal 11: Make Cities Inclusive, Safe, Resilient, and Sustainable', Sustainable Development Goals website (available at: www.un.org/sustainabledevelopment/cities/, accessed 26 February 2018).

19. N. Kabisch, H. Korn, J. Stadler and A. Bonn (eds), *Nature-Based Solutions to Climate Change Adaptation in Urban Areas: Linkages between Science, Policy and Practice* (Cham: Springer International, 2017).

20. M. White, I. Alcock, B. Wheeler and M. Depledge, 'Would You Be Happier Living in a Greener Urban Area?: A Fixed-Effects Analysis of Panel Data', *Psycohlogical Science* 24/6 (2013): 920–928.

21. C. Mercer, C. Scott, K. Pringle *et al.*, 'A Brief Guide of the Benefits of Urban Green Spaces', joint publication of Leeds Ecosystem, Atmosphere and Forest (LEAF) centre, United Bank of Carbon (UBoC), and University of Leeds Sustainable Cities Group (available at: www.leaf.leeds.ac.uk/wp-content/uploads/2015/10/

LEAF_benefits_of_urban_green_space_2015_upd.pdf, accessed 26 February 2018).

22. S. Wachter, 'What is a Tree Worth?: Green-City Strategies, Signaling and Housing Prices', *Real Estate Economics* 36/2 (2008): 213–239.

23. M. Kinver, 'Green Spaces "Can save NHS Billions"', *BBC News*, 6 November 2013 (available at: www.bbc.co.uk/news/science-environment-24806994?, accessed 26 February 2018).

24. P. Newman, T. Beatley and H. Boyer, *Resilient Cities: Responding to Peak Oil and Climate Change* (Washington, DC: Island Press, 2009).

25. P. Sutton and D. Spratt, *Climate Code Red: The Case for Emergency Action* (Melbourne: Scribe Publications, 2008).

26. P. Hawken (ed.), *Drawdown: The Most Comprehensive Plan Ever Proposed to Reverse Global Warming* (London: Penguin, 2018).

27. Amdavad Municipal Corporation, 'Ahmedabad Heat Action Plan 2016: Guide to Extreme Heat Planning in Ahmedabad, India' (available at: www.nrdc.org/sites/default/files/ahmedabad-heat-action-plan-2016.pdf, accessed 26 February 2018).

28. E.O. Wilson, *Biophilia* (Cambridge, MA: Harvard University Press, 1986).

29. J. Harman, *The Shark's Paintbrush: Biomimicry and How Nature is Inspiring Innovation* (Ashland, OR: White Cloud Press, 2013).

30. W. Browning, C. Ryan and J. Clancy, '14 Patterns of Biophilic Design: Improving Health & Well-Being in the Built Environment', report, Terrapin Bright Green LLC (2014) (available at: www.terrapinbrightgreen.com/report/14-patterns/, accessed 26 February 2018).

31. T. Beatley, *Biophilic Cities: Integrating Nature into Urban Design and Planning* (Washington, DC: Island Press, 2011).

32. D. Holmgren, *Permaculture: Principles and Pathways Beyond Sustainability* (Hepburn, VIC: Holmgren Design Services, 2002).

33. T. Hemenway, *The Permaculture City: Regenerative Design for Urban, Suburban, and Town Resilience* (White River Junction, VT: Chelsea Green Publishing, 2015).

34. T. Beatley, *Handbook of Biophilic City Planning & Design* (Washington, DC: Island Press, 2017).

35. J. Benyus, *Biomimicry: Innovation Inspired by Nature* (New York: HarperCollins, 1997).

36. See CEEIBOS website (available at: en.ceebios.com, accessed 1 March 2018).

37. G. Keeffe, 'Synergetic City: Urban Algae Production as a Regenerative Tool for a Post-Industrial City', working paper, International Federation for Housing and Planning Summit, Berlin, 2009 (available at: www.gregkeeffe.co.uk/gregkeeffe/Research_files/gregkeeffe-synergeticcity.pdf, accessed 1 March 2018).

38. A. Bernett, 'Biomimicry Versus Biophilia: What's the Difference?', Terrapin Bright Green Blog, 14 February 2017 (available at: www.terrapinbrightgreen.com/blog/2017/02/biomimicry-versus-biophilia/, accessed 1 March 2018).

39. T.A.M. Pugh, A.R. MacKenzie, J.D. Whyatt and C.N. Hewitt, 'Effectiveness of Green Infrastructure for Improvement of Air Quality in Urban Street Canyons', *Environmental Science & Technology* 46/14 (2012): 7692–7699.

40. See Friends of The High Line website (available at: www.thehighline.org, accessed 1 March 2018).

41. Greater London Authority, 'All London Green Grid', 2018 (available at: www.london.gov.uk/what-we-do/environment/parks-green-spaces-and-biodiversity/all-london-green-grid, accessed 1 March 2018).

42. A. Abdullah, 'Sinagpore Park Connectors Reach 300km at 25-Year Mark', *The Straits Times Singapore*, 21 September 2015 (available at: www.straitstimes.com/singapore/singapore-park-connectors-reach-300km-at-25-year-mark, accessed 1 March 2018).

43. L. Grozdanic, 'The World's Largest Vertical Garden Blooms with 85,000 Plants in the Heart of Bogota', Inhabitat weblog, 5 December 2017 (available at: www.inhabitat.com/the-worlds-largest-vertical-garden-blooms-with-85000-plants-in-the-heart-of-bogota/, accessed 1 March 2018).

44. Stefano Boeria Architetti, 'Vertical Forest', 2009–2014 (available at: www.stefanoboeriarchitetti.net/en/portfolios/vertical-forest/, accessed 1 March 2018).

45. Stefano Boeri Architetti, 'Nanjing Vertical Forest', 2016–2018 (available at: www.stefanoboeriarchitetti.net/en/portfolios/nanjing-vertical-forest/, accessed 1 March 2018).

46. International Living Future Institute, 'Biophilic Design Initiative', 2018 (available at: living-future.org/biophilic-design-overview/, accessed 1 March 2018).

47. See Bullitt Center website (available at: www.bullittcenter.org, accessed 1 March 2018).

48. Arup, 'Cities Alive' (available at: www.arup.com/publications/research/section/cities-alive-rethinking-green-infrastructure, 2016, accessed 1 March 2018).

49. Labmate, 'Termite Technology to Shape New "Breathing" Buildings', 2013 (available at: www.labmate-online.com/news/air-clean-up/16/university_of_nottingham/termite_technology_to_shape_new_breathing_buildings/25262, accessed 1 March 2018).

50. 'Smart Material Houses: BIQ', International Building Exhibition IBA Hamburg 2006–2013 (available at: www.iba-hamburg.de/en/themes-projects/the-building-exhibition-within-the-building-exhibition/smart-material-houses/biq/projekt/biq.html, accessed 1 March 2018).

51. See Blue-Green Cities Research Project website (available at: www.bluegreencities.ac.uk, accessed 1 March 2018).

52. A. Viljoen (ed.), *Continuous Productive Urban Landscapes: Designing Urban Architecture for Sustainable Cities* (Oxford: Architectural Press, 2005).

53. See The Michigan Urban Farming Initiative website (available at: www.miufi.org/, accessed 1 March 2018).

54. See R-Urban website (available at: www.r-urban.net/en/, accessed 1 March 2018).

55. See Farm Fresh To You website (available at: www.farmfreshtoyou.com/, accessed 1 March 2018).

56. E. Henderson, 'Keynote for Urgenci Kobe Conference 2010: "Community Supported Foods and Farming" February 22nd 2010' (available at: urgenci.net/csa-history/, accessed 1 March 2018).

57. T. Donovan, *Feral Cities: Adventures with Animals in the Urban Jungle* (Chicago, IL: Chicago Review Press, 2015).

58. G. Ceballos, P. Erlich, A. Barnosky *et al.*, 'Accellerated Modern Human-Induced Species Loss: Entering the Sixth Mass Extinction', *Science Advances* 1/5 (2015): e1400253 (available at: advances.sciencemag.org/content/1/5/e1400253, accessed 2 March 2018).

59. S. Carver, 'Mapping Rewilding', *Geographical*, 23 November 2015 (available at: www.geographical.co.uk/places/mapping/item/1404-mapping-rewilding, accessed 2 March 2018).

4. THE COMMON CITY

1. R. Florida, *The New Urban Crisis: How Our Cities Are Increasing Inequality, Deepening Segregation, and Failing the Middle Class –*

And What We Can Do about It (London: Hachette, 2017); and L. Wacquant, *Urban Outcasts: A Comparative Sociology of Advanced Marginality* (Cambridge: Polity Press, 2008).

2. M. Davidson and K. Ward (eds), *Cities under Austerity: Restructuring the US Metropolis* (New York: SUNY Press, 2018); and B. Schönig and S. Schipper, *Urban Austerity: Impacts of the Global Financial Crisis on Cities in Europe* (Berlin: Theater der Zeit, 2016).

3. D. Harvey, *A Brief History of Neoliberalism* (Oxford: Oxford University Press, 2007).

4. C. Pollitt and G. Bouckaert, *Public Management Reform: A Comparative Analysis – New Public Management, Governance, and the Neo-Weberian State* (Oxford: Oxford University Press, 2011).

5. J. Peck, N. Theodore and N. Brenner, 'Neoliberal Urbanism Redux?', *International Journal of Urban and Regional Research* 37/3 (2013): 1091–1099; and B. Jessop, 'Liberalism, Neoliberalism, and Urban Governance: A State Theoretical Perspective', *Antipode* 34/3 (2002): 452–472.

6. D. Harvey, 'From Managerialism to Entrepreneurialism: The Transformation in Urban Governance in Late Capitalism', *Geografiska Annaler B* 71/1 (1989): 3–17.

7. UN, 'The World's Cities in 2016: Data Booklet' (available at: www.un.org/en/development/desa/population/publications/pdf/ urbanization/the_worlds_cities_in_2016_data_booklet.pdf, accessed 6 March 2018).

8. UN-HABITAT, *State of the World's Cities 2010/2011 – Cities for All: Bridging the Urban Divide 2010* (London: Earthscan, 2008) (available at: mirror.unhabitat.org/pmss/listItemDetails. aspx?publicationID=2917, accessed 6 March 2018).

9. A. Simms, P. Kjell and R. Potts, 'Clone Town Britain: The Survey Results on the Bland State of the Nation', report (London: New Economics Foundation, 2005) (available at: www.neweconomics. org/2007/06/clone-town-britain/, accessed 6 March 2018).

10. S. Sassen, 'Who Owns Our Cities – and Why this Urban Takeover Should Concern Us All', *The Guardian*, 24 November 2015 (available at: www.theguardian.com/cities/2015/nov/24/who-owns-our-cities-and-why-this-urban-takeover-should-concern-us-all, accessed 6 March 2018).

11. L. Lees, T. Slater and E. Wyly, *Gentrification* (London: Routledge, 2007).

12. C. Crouch, *Post-Democracy* (Cambridge: Polity Press, 2004).

13. The POWER Inquiry, 'Power to the People – The report of Power: An Independent Inquiry into Britain's Democracy', The centenary project of the Joseph Rowntree Charitable Trust and the Joseph Rowntree Reform Trust, 2006 (available at: www.jrrt.org.uk/sites/jrrt.org.uk/files/documents/PowertothePeople_001.pdf, accessed 6 March 2018).

14. K. Cahill, *Who Owns Britain and Ireland: The Hidden Facts Behind Landownership in the UK and Ireland* (Edinburgh: Canongate Books, 2001).

15. A. Moore, 'Who Owns Almost All America's Land?', Research & Commentary – Inequality, 15 February 2016 (available at: www.inequality.org/research/owns-land/, accessed 6 March 2018).

16. O. Wainwright, 'Britain has Enough Land to Solve the Housing Crisis – It's Just Being Hoarded', *The Guardian*, 31 January 2017 (available at: www.theguardian.com/cities/2017/jan/31/britain-land-housing-crisis-developers-not-building-land-banking, accessed 6 March 2018).

17. M. Mayer, C. Thörn and H. Thörn (eds), *Urban Uprisings: Challenging Neoliberal Urbanism in Europe* (London: Palgrave Macmillan, 2016).

18. V. Shiva, *Biopiracy: The Plunder of Nature and Knowledge* (San Francisco, CA: South End Press, 1997); M. Hardt and A. Negri, *Commonwealth* (Cambridge, MA: Harvard University Press, 2009); P. Linebaugh, *The Magna Carta Manifesto: Liberties and Common for All* (Berkeley, CA: University of California Press, 2008); and D. Bollier, *Think Like a Commoner: A Short Introduction to the Life of the Common* (Gabriola Island, BC: New Society Publishers, 2014).

19. D. Patti and L. Polyák (eds), *Funding the Cooperative City: Community Finance and the Economy of Civic Spaces* (Vienna: Cooperative City Books, 2017).

20. Power to Change, 'Ground-Breaking £8 Million Programme to Tackle Inequality at Local Level Announced', 2017 (available at: www.powertochange.org.uk/news/ground-breaking-8-million-programme-tackle-inequality-local-level-announced/, accessed 6 March 2018).

21. Locality, 'Locality Strategy 2015–2020', London, April 2015 (available at: locality.org.uk/wp-content/uploads/Locality-strategy-2015-2020-FINAL-high-res-images.pdf, accessed 6 March 2018).

22. Plunkett Foundation, 'Cooperative Pubs', 2017 (available at: www.plunkett.co.uk/cooperative-pubs, accessed 6 March 2018).

23. Scottish Housing News, 'More than 500,000 acres of land in Scotland Now Under Community Ownership', 2017 (available at: www.scottishhousingnews.com/18875/more-than-500000-acres-of-land-in-scotland-now-under-community-ownership/, accessed 6 March 2018).

24. World Habitat Awards, 'Caño Martín Peña Community Land Trust', 2015 (available at: www.world-habitat.org/world-habitat-awards/winners-and-finalists/cano-martin-pena-community-land-trust/, accessed 6 March 2018).

25. C. Reed, 'Dutch Nursing Home Offers Rent-Free Housing to Students', *PBS New Hour*, 5 April 2015 (available at: www.pbs.org/newshour/world/dutch-retirement-home-offers-rent-free-housing-students-one-condition, accessed 6 March 2018).

26. L. Tummers, 'The Re-Emergence of Self-Managed Co-Housing in Europe: A Critical Review of Co-Housing Research', *Urban Studies* 53/10 (2016): 2023–2040.

27. LILAC website (available at: www.lilac.coop, accessed 6 March 2018). P. Chatterton, 'Towards an Agenda for Post-Carbon Cities: Lessons from Lilac, the UK's First Ecological, Affordable Cohousing Community', *International Journal of Urban and Regional Research* 37/5 (2013): 1654–1674.

28. See Startblock Reikerhaven website (available at: www.startblok.amsterdam/en/, accessed 6 March 2018).

29. M. Mean, C. White, and E. Lasota, 'We Can Make: Civic Innovation in Housing', report (Bristol: Knowle West Media Centre and White Design, 2017) (available at: kwmc.org.uk/projects/wecanmake/, accessed 6 March 2018).

30. A. Pittini and W. Laino, 'Housing Europe Review 2012: The Nuts and Bolts of European Social Housing Systems', report (Brussels: ECODHAS Housing Europe's Observatory, 2011) (available at: www.housingeurope.eu/resource-105/the-housing-europe-review-2012, accessed 6 March 2018).

31. J.E. Hardoy and D. Satterthwaite, *Squatter Citizen: Life in the Urban Third World* (London: Earthscan, 2013).

32. A. Heywood, 'Local Housing, Community Living: Prospects for Scaling Up and Scaling Out Community-Led Housing', report (London: The Smith Institute, 2016) (available at: www.

smith-institute.org.uk/wp-content/uploads/2016/02/local-housing-community-living.pdf, accessed 6 March 2018).

33. W. Wilson, 'Self-Build and Custom Build Housing (England)', House of Common Briefing Paper no. 06784, 2017 (available at: http://researchbriefings.parliament.uk/ResearchBriefing/Summary/SN06784, accessed 6 March 2018).

34. Ministry of Housing, Communities and Local Government and A. Sharma MP, 'Launch of the UK's First Plot Shop in Bicester, Oxfordshire', press release, 2017 (available at: www.gov.uk/government/news/launch-of-the-uks-first-plot-shop, accessed 6 March 2018).

35. See DemoDev website (available at: www.demodev.org, accessed 6 March 2018).

36. E.F. Schumacher, *Small is Beautiful: A Study of Economics As If People Mattered* (London: Blond & Briggs, 1973); R. Douthwaite, *The Growth Illusion: How Economic Growth has Enriched the Few, Impoverished the Many and Endangered the Planet* (Dublin: Lilliput Press, 1993); H. Daly, *Beyond Growth: The Economics of Sustainable Development* (Boston: Beacon Press, 1996); and J. Blewitt and R. Cunningham (eds), *Post-Growth Project: How the End of Economic Growth Could Bring a Fairer and Happier Society* (London: Green House Publishing, 2014). Organisations such as The Post Growth Institute have also been established to support these ideas. See www.postgrowth.org, accessed 6 March 2018).

37. See, for example, G. Kallis, *Degrowth* (New York: Columbia University Press, 2018); G. D'Alisa, F. Demaria and G. Kallis (eds), *Degrowth: A Vocabulary for a New Era* (London: Routledge, 2015); and D. O'Neill, 'A Sustainable Economy', Progressive Economies Group Policy Brief, 2017 (available at: www.peg.primeeconomics.org/policybriefs/a-sustainable-economy. accessed 6 March 2018).

38. T. Jackson, *Prosperity without Growth: Economics for a Finite Planet* (London: Earthscan, 2011).

39. Green New Deal Group, 'A National Plan for the UK: From Austerity to the Age of the Green New Deal', Fifth Anniversary Report of the Green New Deal Group (New Weather Institute, 2013) (available at: www.greennewdealgroup.org/wp-content/uploads/2013/09/Green-New-Deal-5th-Anniversary.pdf, accessed 6 March 2018).

40. P. Mason, *Post-Capitalism: A Guide to Our Future* (London: Penguin, 2016).

41. J. Schor, *Plenitude: The New Economics of True Wealth* (London: Penguin, 2010).

42. K. Raworth, *Doughnut Economics: Seven Ways to Think Like a 21st-Century Economist* (London: Random House Business, 2018).

43. P.A. Lawn, 'A Theoretical Foundation to Support the Index of Sustainable Economic Welfare (ISEW), Genuine Progress Indicator (GPI), and Other Related Indexes', *Ecological Economics* 44/1 (2003): 105–118.

44. Happy City, 'Thriving Places Index: A Very New Measure of Progress', 2016 (available at: www.happycity.org.uk/measurement-policy/happy-city-index/, accessed 6 March 2018).

45. J.K. Gibson-Graham, *The End of Capitalism (As We Knew It)*, 2nd edn (Minneapolis: University of Minnesota Press, 2006) ; J.K. Gibson-Graham J-K and J. Cameron J, *Take Back the Economy: An Ethical Guide for Transforming Our Communities* (Minneapolis, MN: University of Minnesota Press, 2013); and J.K. Gibson-Graham, *A Postcapitalist Politics* (Minneapolis, MN: University of Minnesota Press, 2006).

46. A. Bowman, I. Ertürk, J. Froud *et al.*, *The End of the Experiment?: From Competition to the Foundational Economy* (Manchester: Manchester University Press, 2014).

47. See the Next System Project website (available at: thenextsystem. org, accessed 6 March 2018).

48. Cooperatives UK, 'The UK Cooperative Economy 2012: Alternatives to Austerity', report (Manchester: Cooperatives UK, 2012) (available at: http://image.guardian.co.uk/sys-files/Society/documents/2012/06/27/UKcooperativeeconomoy2012.pdf, accessed 6 March 2018).

49. W.F. Whyte and K.K. Whyte, *Making Mondragón: The Growth and Dynamics of the Worker Cooperative Complex*, Cornell International Industrial and Labor Relations Report no. 14, 2nd edn (Ithaca, NY: ILR Press, 1991).

50. S. Matthews, 'Catalan Solidarity: Frustration to Transformation', *Stir to Action*, Winter 2017 (available at: www.stirtoaction.com/issues/issue-16, accessed 6 March 2018).

51. Cooperation Jackson, 'The Community Production Initiative' (available at: www.cooperationjackson.org/the-community-production-initiative/, accessed 6 March 2018).

52. A.P. Marshall and D.W. O'Neill, 'The Bristol Pound: A Tool for Localisation?', *Ecological Economics* 146 (2018): 273–281; and P. North, *Local Money* (Cambridge: Green Books, 2010).

53. See Ithaca HOURS website (available at: www.ithacahours.com, accessed 6 March 2018).

54. D. Boyle, 'More than Money: Platforms for Exchange and Reciprocity in Public Services', discussion paper (London: nef and NESTA, 2011) (available at: www.nesta.org.uk/sites/default/files/more_than_money.pdf, accessed 6 March 2018).

55. Brixton Pound, 'What is the Brixton Pound?' (available at: www.brixtonpound.org/what, accessed 6 March 2018).

56. A. Howarth, 'Economic Adviser Backs Scottish Government's Basic Income Plans', *The Scotsman*, 7 January 2018 (available at: www.scotsman.com/news/economic-adviser-backs-scottish-government-s-basic-income-plans-1-4655527, accessed 6 March 2018); and Kela, 'Basic Income Experiment 2017–2018' (available at: www.kela.fi/web/en/basic-income-experiment-2017-2018, accessed 6 March 2018).

57. D. Azzellini, 'Labour as a Common: The Example of Worker-Recuperated Companies', *Critical Sociology* (2016): 1–14.

58. P. North and M. Scott Cato (eds), *Towards Just and Sustainable Economies: The Social and Solidarity Economy North and South* (Bristol: Policy Press, 2016).

59. See the New Citizenship Project website (available at: www.newcitizenship.org.uk, accessed 6 March 2018).

60. C. Ward, *Social Policy: An Anarchist Response* (London: Freedom Press, 2000).

61. B. Barber, *Strong Democracy* (San Francisco, CA: University of California Press, 1984).

62. See the People's Plan Greater Manchester website (available at: www.peoplesplangm.org.uk, accessed 6 March 2018).

63. Citizens Foundation, 'Better Reykjavik', 2010 (available at: www.citizens.is/portfolio_page/better_reykjavik/, accessed 6 March 2018).

64. Participatory Budgeting Project, 'Participatory Budgeting in North America, 2014–2015: A Year of Growth' (available at: www.participatorybudgeting.org/participatory-budgeting-in-north-america-2014-2015-a-year-of-growth/, accessed 6 March 2018).

152 · UNLOCKING SUSTAINABLE CITIES

65. R. Patel, 'Participatory Budgeting: It's Not What You Do, It's How You Do It', *RSA*, 7 November 2016 (available at: www. thersa.org/discover/publications-and-articles/rsa-blogs/2016/11/ participatory-budgeting-its-not-what-you-do---its-how-you-do-it, accessed 6 March 2018).

66. R. Oldenburg, *The Great Good Place: Cafes, Coffee Shops, Bookstores, Bars, Hair Salons, and Other Hangouts at the Heart of a Community* (New York: Marlowe & Co., 1999).

67. See European Network of Living Labs website (available at: www. openlivinglabs.eu/, accessed 6 March 2018).

68. See the Participatory City Foundation website (available at: www. participatorycity.org/, accessed 6 March 2018).

69. M. Horton and P. Freire, *We make the Road by Walking: Conversations on Education and Social Change*, edited by B. Bell, J. Gaventa and J. Peters (Philadelphia, PA: Temple University Press, 1990); and P. Freire, *The Pedagogy of the Oppressed* (London: Penguin, 1996).

70. M. Rosenberg, *Nonviolent Communication: A Language of Life*, 3rd edn (Encinitas, CA: PuddleDancer Press, 2015).

71. B. Robertson, *Holacracy: The Revolutionary Management System that Abolishes Hierarchy* (London: Penguin, 2016); and G. Endenburg, *Sociocracy: The Organization of Decision Making* (Delft: Eburon, 2002).

72. P. Chatterton and S. Hodkinson, 'Autonomy in the City? Reflections on the Social Centres Movement in the UK', *City* 10/3 (2006): 305–315.

73. Khora (XΩPA), 'About Us' (available at: www.khora-athens.org/ organisation/, accessed 6 March 2018).

5. THINK BIG, ACT SMALL, START NOW

1. C. Ratti and M. Claudel, *The City of Tomorrow: Sensors, Networks, Hackers, and the Future of Urban Life* (New Haven, CT: Yale University Press, 2016).

2. J. Holloway, *In, Against and Beyond Capitalism: The San Francisco Lectures* (Oakland, CA: PM Press, 2016); and E.O. Wright, *Envisioning Real Utopias* (New York: Verso, 2010).

3. D.K. Leach, 'Prefigurative Politics', in D.A. Snow, D. della Porta, B. Klandermans and D. MacAdam (eds), *The Wiley-Blackwell*

Encyclopedia of Social and Political Movements (Oxford: Blackwell, 2013) DOI: 10.1002/9780470674871.wbespm167.

4. B. Bond and Z. Exley, *Rules for Revolutionaries: How Big Organizing Can Change Everything* (White River Junction, VT: Chelsea Green Publishing, 2016).

5. R. Mackay and A. Avanessian (eds), *#Accelerate: The Accelerationist Reader* (Falmouth: Urbanomic Media, 2014).

6. A. Cumbers, *Reclaiming Public Ownership: Making Space for Economic Democracy* (London: Zed Books, 2012).

7. T. Fry, *Remaking Cities: Introduction to Urban Metrofitting* (London: Bloomsbury, 2017).

8. Frost and Sullivan, 'Strategic Opportunity Analysis of the Global Smart City Market', consulting report (available at: www.egr.msu.edu/~aesc310-web/resources/SmartCities/Smart%20City%20Market%20Report%202.pdf, accessed 6 March 2018).

9. The exact origin of this quote is unclear, but according to Wiki quotes it was expressed during the programme: 'The Science in Science Fiction', on NPR's *Talk of the Nation*, 30 November 1999 (Timecode 11:55).

10. T. Bliss, 'Urbalism: The Development of Resilient Outside-In Cities', (available at: https://urbalblog.wordpress.com/urbalism/, accessed 6 March 2018).

11. See V. Welter, *Biopolis: Patrick Geddes and the City of Life* (Stanford, CA: MIT Press, 2003); P. Kropotkin, *Fields, Factories and Workshops* (London: Freedom Press, 1998); and E. Howard, *Garden Cities of To-Morrow* (London: Attic Press, 1985).

12. S. Graham (ed.), *Cities, War, and Terrorism: Towards an Urban Geopolitics* (Oxford: Blackwell, 2004).

13. Fry, *Remaking Cities*.

14. G. Deleuze and F. Guattari, *A Thousand Plateaus* (London: Continuum, 2004).

15. See Fungi Perfecti® website, 'About Paul Stamets' (available at: www.fungi.com/about-paul-stamets.html, accessed 6 March 2018).

Index

The Pluto Press Newsletter

Hello friend of Pluto!

Want to stay on top of the best radical books
we publish?

Then sign up to be the first to hear about our
new books, as well as special events,
podcasts and videos.

You'll also get 50% off your first order with us
when you sign up.

Come and join us!

Go to bit.ly/PlutoNewsletter